Pillows, Cushions and Tuffets

Carol Zentgraf

Published by

kp krause publications
An F&W Publications Company

700 East State Street • Iola, WI 54990-0001
715-445-2214 • 888-457-2873
www.krause.com

To place an order or obtain a free catalog, please call 800-258-0929.

Library of Congress Catalog Number 2003114959
ISBN 0-87349-693-0

Edited by Christine Townsend
Designed by Becky Robinson
Printed in the United States of America

DEDICATION

I'd like to dedicate this book to my husband Dave, and our children Dan and Carolyn, for their love and continuing support of my creative endeavors.

FOREWORD

Quite frankly, when Carol told me she was doing a book that included tuffets, I had to go to the dictionary for clarification, as the only reference I had for this word was the nursery rhyme, "Little Miss Muffet." Until reading this book manuscript, I had no idea of the excitement this decorator piece could bring to a room.

Pillows are always a source of comfort for snuggling in on a rainy day, or for support while watching a late-night movie. From a decorating perspective, use them as a means to introduce a spark of pizzazz into a mundane room's color palette. One can never have too many of them (like the wonderful fabrics they're made from). I'm sure Linus would have much rather had a soft pillow than a blanket!

In this book, *Pillows, Cushions and Tuffets*, Carol has made the most complex looking details easy to create with simple, step-by-step instructions. Even matching those challenging, uneven stripes becomes a piece of cake if you follow her words.

As long as I've known Carol–through her work on *Sew News, Sewing Décor*, and other published works–I've thought of her as a home dec pro with a great sense of style, and the ability to write directions anyone can follow ... and this book is one more work that reinforces my opinion.

Have fun creating these decorator accents for every room in your home!

-Linda Griepentrog
Sew News editor

Acknowledgments

This book has been a pleasure to write, and I couldn't have done it without the support and assistance of a great group of individuals and companies. I'd like to acknowledge and thank the artisans and companies listed in the Credits on page 126 for generously supplying the products used, and give a big thanks to the following individuals:

First of all, to my husband Dave, for living amidst a sea of fabrics, then pillows, cushions, and tuffets that took over our home, and for never minding when the only activity in the kitchen involved sewing. Also to my talented and creative daughter, Carolyn, who came home from college for her summer break and hit the door sewing cushions and covering chair seats. And to my mother, Carolyn Ryan, for her always-cheerful support and for spending a week at my house cutting fabric non-stop.

To my long-time friend and Krause acquisitions editor, Julie Stephani, for her encouragement and good advice; to my editor, Christine Townsend, for all of her help; and to the rest of the great group I've worked with at Krause.

To my former boss and sewing mentor, *Sew News* editor Linda Griepentrog, who gave me the opportunity to be part of the textiles and sewing industry, sent me to skill-building seminars, and taught me the finer points of acquiring a fabric stash. Also for giving me permission to feature pillows I made for *Sew News* in this book.

To Annette Bailey, editor of *Creative Machine Embroidery* magazine, for letting me use photos of pillows and a bench from the magazine.

To my friends, Marilyn Howard and Elizabeth Dubicki, for their sewing skills and their pillows that are included in this book; Kari Lee of The Leather Factory for letting me feature a suede tuffet she designed; and fellow Krause author Nancy Cornwell for being a source of encouragement and inspiration.

To the owners and great staff of Jackman's Fabrics in St. Louis, Missouri, who helped me plan the cover projects and tropical grouping and provided the fabrics and trims used for them; to Sew N Sew in Waupaca, Wisconsin, for the use of the Viking Designer I sewing machine which appears in photos in this book, and Hanson's Furniture in Waupaca, Wisconsin, for graciously opening their doors to me. Thanks to the Edler and Stephani families for their generosity.

Introduction

I've always loved decorating, especially with accessories, so this book is a natural culmination of two of my favorite hobbies: decorating and sewing … and painting too, but just a smattering. Making these accessories is all about fun—you can let your imagination run free and just have a good time. The sewing is easy; some projects don't even require a needle or thread, only a minimum amount of fabrics and trims, and you can enjoy the satisfaction of creating something unique. After a long, busy day, you may even discover that there can be something therapeutic about using the staple gun or drill needed for some of the tuffets.

So why pillows, cushions, and tuffets—what do they have in common? For one thing, they can all make any room a more comfortable place to be. After all, everyone loves to sink into a big pile of pillows, relax with their feet on a tuffet or sit on a comfy, cushioned seat. These accessories also add the finishing touches to your décor. They reflect your taste and personality.

If you enjoy looking at decorating magazines or browsing through upscale home furnishings stores, you've probably noticed that many warm and inviting or eye-catching rooms owe at least part of their good looks to accessories. High-end decorating catalogs, too, often feature wonderful—and pricey—pillows and cushions or elaborate tuffets to add a designer look and character to room settings. The good news is you can capture these same looks for a fraction of the cost when you make them yourself. You can also custom-design them to suit your lifestyle and décor. Whether you're looking for an elegant, traditional accent or a fun-loving accessory to add a bit of whimsy, you determine the look with the fabrics and trims you select.

TABLE OF
Contents

CHAPTER 1

Getting Started

Sewing for your home should be enjoyable as well as practical,

and advance planning will ensure both your success and pleasure.

It's important to choose fabrics that will suit your décor and

lifestyle; it's convenient to have the materials you'll need on hand.

So before you begin, take a little time to think about your creative

endeavor, considering which of the following supplies you'll need.

Selecting Fabrics, Trims, and Buttons

This is where the fun begins. A veritable sea of beautiful fabrics, trims, and buttons awaits your sewing pleasure. Of course, the most practical approach to home décor sewing is to decide on a project, then purchase the supplies. But for many sewers, it often works in reverse. A wonderful fabric, spectacular buttons, or unusual trim can provide inspiration to create the project, justifying the amazing fabric and trim stashes owned by many people who love to decorate and sew. Best of all, it doesn't matter if you're a beginner or you've been sewing for years—if you fall in love with a fabric, it's probably meant to be yours.

Fabric

Factors to consider when selecting fabrics are:

■ Where will the finished item be used? The amount of wear the fabric will receive should be a major factor in the selection process. While silk, suede, and other elegant fabrics are beautiful for finished items that won't receive a lot of wear and tear, more durable fabrics are better suited for everyday use. The silk dupioni floor cushions on page 83, for example, are wonderful for a formal setting used by adults. Denim, velveteen, or sturdy cotton home décor fabrics are more practical choices in rooms for younger people.

■ Whether the fabric will be used in the house or outdoors is also an important consideration. Fabrics for outdoor use are either made of water-repellent fibers, such as nylon, or have a water-resistant finish applied to them.

■ Good-quality fabric is usually easier to sew and will hold up better than poorer qualities. Before making a purchase, examine the fabric for a tight, even weave with a high thread count per inch, evenly dyed or printed color, and resiliency (the ability to spring back to shape after you wrinkle it in your hand). Fabrics without these attributes may pull apart at the seams, fade easily, or appear rumpled after a few uses.

■ Exceptions to the tight-weave rule are handwoven, and other fabrics, that are meant to be more loosely woven. Here, the looser weave is part of the fabric's character and appeal.

■ Design and color. These considerations are strictly aesthetic, but important nonetheless. It's always a good idea to see how a fabric looks in your room before purchasing yardage, and most fabric stores or mail-order sources will be happy to provide you with swatches. Or, take a small notebook with other fabrics you're trying to match when you visit the fabric store.

Home Décor/Decorator Fabrics

Usually 54" to 60" wide, these fabrics are suitable for a wide range of decorating projects. They range from sheers to heavyweight upholstery fabrics and are generally the most suitable for large projects such as tuffets, or for cushions and seat covers that will be subjected to wear. Many of these decorator fabrics are available in coordinating collections of large and small prints, checks, stripes, plaids or solids that offer creative options for mixing and matching.

Apparel Fabrics

Many apparel fabrics can also be used for home décor projects, especially pillows and smaller tuffets. Suitable fabrics include silk, velvet, velveteen, denim and other cotton fabrics, real or faux leather and suede, lace, and satin.

Hand-dyed and Handwoven Fabrics

Created by textile artisans, these unique fabrics can be found at quilt and sewing expositions, specialty fabric shops or purchased directly from the artist's studio. See the Resources on page 126.

Linens

Whether vintage or new, handkerchiefs, place mats, table runners, tablecloths, and pillowcases can be used to create unique pillows and other home décor accents. Look for interesting effects such as quilting, embroidery, and decorative edges—showcase those details in your design.

Trims

Trims add finishing touches to pillows, cushions, and tuffets, and impart character as well as a designer look. If you observe expensive accessories in home decorating stores or catalogs, you're likely to see a lavish use of trims.

All trims belong to one of two categories: sew-in or sew-on. Sew-in trims have a flange—or lip—that is functional only and intended to be inserted in a seam as you sew. Sew-on trims don't have a lip at all, or feature one that's decorative and designed to be sewn, fused, or glued onto to the finished project.

Trims commonly used for home décor embellishment are:

■ **Welting.** Welting is a fabric-covered cord with a lip that's used as a sew-in trim for seam finishing and edges. It adds structural stability and design definition to pillows and cushions, as well as other home décor fabrications. It's available pre-made in a limited variety of colors. You can easily make your own welting by covering cotton filler cord with bias-cut fabric strips.

■ **Twisted Cord.** Twisted cord is made of twisted yarn plies that have been twisted together and is available with or with-out a lip. You can find it in a wide variety of colors, usually in ¼" and ⅜" diameter sizes. Cord with a lip is used for seam and edge finishing. Cord without a lip can be used for a variety of embellishment purposes ranging from couching to ties.

■ **Fringe.** Fringe is also available in myriad colors, lengths, and styles. Some fringes come in matching sew-in and decorative-edge styles, while others are offered in one or the other. Fringe can be used for edge and seam finishing, surface embellishments, and for making tassels.

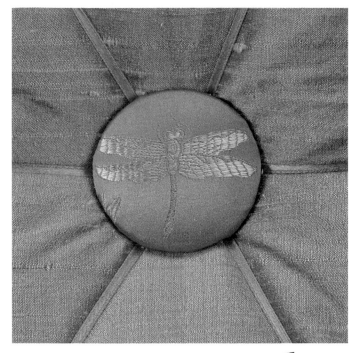

Buttons and Beads

If you've never given much thought to buttons, now is the time to begin noticing the wonderful array of very cool buttons that are available. Ranging from utilitarian to raku, glass, and polymer clay buttons that are works of art, buttons are fun to collect and use.

Buttons and beads can be used for practical purposes like pillow closures or tufting, or as decorative accents for embellishment. Two-part forms are also available for covering with fabric, and are made with the shank on either the inside of the front or the back. Be sure to select forms with the shank on the front to use for tufting; if the shank is on the back, you may pull the back off when you tighten the tuft.

■ **Flat Trims.** Flat trim, gimp, and ribbon feature finished edges on both sides. They are sewn, fused, or glued in place, and are used to cover seams or edges and for decorative surface embellishments.

■ **Novelty Trims.** Novelty trims, such as feathers, decorative yarns, pre-stitched faux chenille, and beaded trims can add a touch of fun to your sewing. Application techniques vary with the trim; consult the manufacturer's instructions or your fabric store sales associate if you're uncertain how to apply the trim.

■ **Tassels.** Tassels can add looks ranging from whimsical to elegant and are available in many colors, lengths, and styles. Some tassels have hanging loops and others are added to cording for chair ties and tiebacks. They can be used to accent pillow centers or corners, as ties to secure a chair cushion or wrap around a pillow, or simply as a decorative accent to hang from a tuffet. You can also make your own tassels using fringe, yarn, fabric strips, or embroidery floss.

Supplies, Tools, and Notions

In addition to basic sewing supplies, you'll need filler materials such as pillow forms, batting, polyester fiberfill or upholstery foam for the projects in this book. Zippers and upholstery supplies are also necessary as indicated in the project instructions. The other tools and notions featured here are optional, but I guarantee you'll be glad you have them. They can save you time, reduce frustration, improve your sewing skills—and generally make your life easier.

Filler Materials

Pillow forms are readily available in square, round, rectangular, and bolster shapes in a variety of sizes. For sizes or special shapes that aren't available, you can make your own by sewing two layers of muslin together and stuffing them with polyester fiberfill.

Upholstery foam is available in sheets sold by the inch from ½"- to 6"-thick, or as 1"- to 2"-thick prepackaged cushions. Poly-fil® Nu-Foam® is a compressed polyester alternative to upholstery foam that doesn't hold water or disintegrate and resists mildew, making it ideal for outdoor cushions as well as indoor fabrications.

Batting is used to lightly pad a surface or to layer over upholstery foam for a smoother surface. Cotton batting is usually a thin, dense sheet and polyester batting is available in a range of lofts.

Upholstery Supplies

Upholsterer's needles have a large eye, are very sturdy and used for tufting, sewing on buttons, or hand sewing curved surfaces. They're available as long, straight needles or curved needles in a range of lengths.

Waxed button thread is ideal for tufting and securely sewing buttons. This heavyweight thread knots securely and will not break during stitching.

Upholstery zippers are heavier in weight than regular zippers and used for projects like seat cushions. They are available in pre-cut lengths or by the yard.

Marking Tools

Chalk markers, tailor's chalk, and water- or heat-soluble fabric markers and pencils are essential tools for accurate sewing and embellishing. However, some work better on certain fabrics: Always test the marker on a fabric scrap first.

Pillow Templates

If you plan to make a lot of pillows, you'll love these pillow templates. Made of a heavyweight transparent material, these templates are designed for marking the outline of panels, and make it easy to center a fabric motif.

The Standard Pillow Template can be used to mark square, rectangular, or round panels with square corners, in sizes ranging from 10" to 24". Measurements are in 1" intervals and seam allowances aren't included.

The Tapered Corner Pillow Template is designed for marking square or rectangular panels with tapered corners and can be used for panels ranging from 11" to 30". It's marked with measurements in 1" intervals that include ½" seam allowances. *Note:* Tapering prevents the pillow corners from being floppy; also see "General Techniques" to mark square corners for tapering. Look for these templates at fabric stores, or see the Resources on page 126 to order them.

Basting Tape and Fabric Adhesives

Wash-A-Way Wonder Tape®, distributed by Dritz, is one of my favorite sewing notions. This self-adhesive, double-sided basting tape eliminates the need for pins and prevents the fabric layers from shifting as you sew. It's also great for securing zipper seam allowances or trims while you sew them. The tape is water-soluble and can be removed with a damp cloth or by machine washing.

Fusible adhesive sheets and tapes are also convenient for myriad sewing needs. Lightweights are ideal for fusing hems and adhering trims, appliqués, or fabric panels that will be sewn in place. Heavier weights offer a more secure bond that doesn't require sewing, but add stiffness to the fabric. Always follow the manufacturer's instructions when using these products.

Fabri-Tac™ Permanent Adhesive for fabric from Beacon™ is another favorite notion of mine. It's great for adhering trims of all weights without adding stiffness and can also be used for making quick repairs to seams or for gluing an entire seam. It adheres to wood, metal and foam, as well as fabric and leather, making it especially useful for projects like tuffets with unlike surfaces.

Measuring and Cutting Tools

Clear, gridded rulers, yardsticks, and squares are ideal for accurate measuring, determining angles, and for use with a rotary cutter. They are available in a variety of sizes. Omnigrid also offers a circle-marking guide that works in conjunction with their gridded yardstick. A convenient guide for measuring and setting seam widths and hem depths up to 6" is the Hem Guide® and Seam Guide® from the Dritz Interior Expressions line.

A rotary cutter makes quick work of cutting fabric panels. Use a straight blade for most cutting purposes or a decorative blade for special effects on non-fraying fabrics. These cutters are razor-sharp, so choose one with a blade that retracts when it's not in use.

A gridded cutting mat is a necessity if you're using a rotary cutter, and a convenient measuring surface even if you're using scissors. These mats are available in assorted sizes—my favorite is a large 33" x 58" mat that accommodates the entire width of a home décor fabric. June Tailor also offers a convenient portable cutting mat with a padded ironing surface on the reverse side. I like to keep this near my sewing machine for quick cutting or pressing needs; it's also a great pinning and measuring surface for making the faux chenille fringe on page 39, or for making your own tassels or fringe.

Other Tools

Fasturn® Tube Turning Tools make turning fabric tubes for ties a breeze. A set of these tools comes with a range of sizes suitable for any tie width you'd like to make.

For making tuffets, you will also need a medium-tip permanent marker for marking foam, a drill for making holes for tufting, a heavy-duty staple gun, a heavy-duty craft knife or box cutter for cutting Nu-Foam, and an electric knife for cutting upholstery foam.

Specialty Sewing Machine Feet

Any job is easier when you use tools specifically designed for the task, and sewing is no exception. In addition to standard and zipper feet, other feet are available for many sewing machines. Specialty machine feet can make techniques such as gathering, making, and attaching ruffles, couching cord or braid, sewing welting and hemming a breeze to stitch. Check your sewing machine manual or consult your dealer for feet available for your machine.s and cording, and for attaching cording or welting to the fabric.

Cord Foot. Designed for couching yarn and narrow cord or trim to the fabric surface, this foot features a guide for the trim. Simply mark a line for your trim design on the fabric surface, feed the trim into the foot, then stitch along the marked line.

Welt Cord Foot. This foot has a cut out groove on the underside that rides along the cording and allows you to stitch closer to the edge than you can with most zipper feet. It's great for making welting with fabric strip

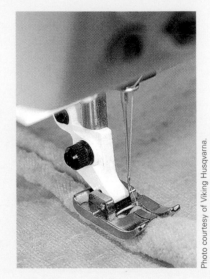

Photo courtesy of Viking Husqvarna.

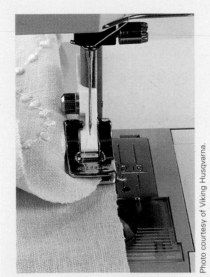

Photo courtesy of Viking Husqvarna.

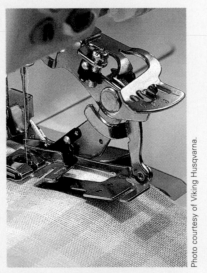

Photo courtesy of Viking Husqvarna.

Photo courtesy of Viking Husqvarna.

Gathering Foot. This foot can either gather fabric only, or can gather and sew it to another fabric simultaneously. It's ideal for gathering tuffet skirts or for gathering and attaching ruffles to pillow or cushion panels.

Ruffler. A ruffler allows you to make even pleats or gathers. You can set the spacing as you desire. It's useful for the same applications as the gathering foot.

Hem Foot. Available for several rolled hem depths, this foot enables you to roll and stitch a hem in light- to medium-weight fabrics.

CHAPTER 2

General Techniques

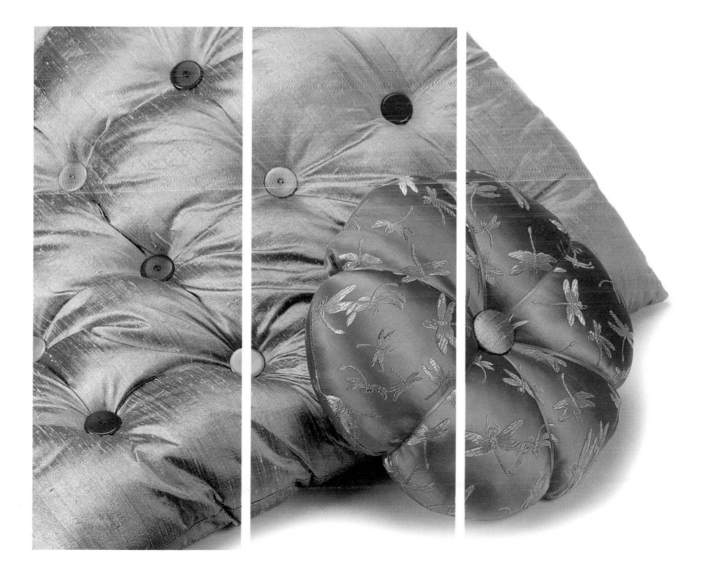

Taking Measurements

To ensure the best possible fit, it's important to measure the actual pillow or cushion form to be covered. The dimensions given on the form packaging may vary slightly, resulting in a too-small or large cover if you base cutting on that information only. Measure the form from seam to seam as shown.

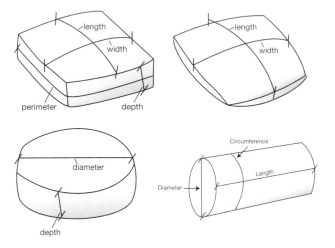

Determining Yardage

To make pillows, cushions or tuffets of any size, you will need to know the measurements of the fabric pieces to be used, adding ½" to each edge for a seam allowance. For tuffets, decide the top surface measurements and add the depth of the foam and board to be covered, plus several inches to allow for stapling in place.

To determine the trim yardage, boxing strip length or finished ruffle length needed to go around square or rectangular panels, add the length of the four sides to determine the perimeter; add 2" for an overlap or seam allowance. For a round panel, multiply the diameter of the circle by 3.14 to determine the circumference of the panel; add 2" for an overlap or seam allowance.

Materials Needed

The instructions for each project in this book are accompanied by the project's finished size and the materials needed to make that size. To make the project in a different size, adjust the form size and fabric and trim yardage accordingly.

In addition to the materials listed, you will also need matching sewing thread, scissors, and straight pins.

Pattern Making and Cutting

Shaped Cushions

To make a pattern for a chair or stool with a shaped surface:

1 Place a sheet of pattern tracing cloth or freezer paper on the seat and draw around the edges, indicating any spokes where the cushion will be tied.

2 Remove the pattern, add a ½" seam allowance all around, and cut out.

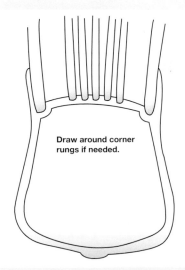
Draw around corner rungs if needed.

Circles

There are several ways to draft circles for round stool cushions, pillows, or tuffets.

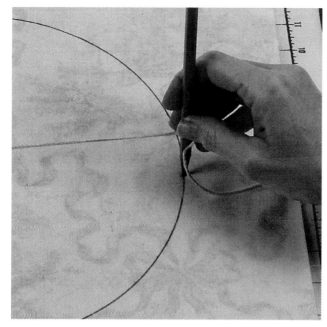

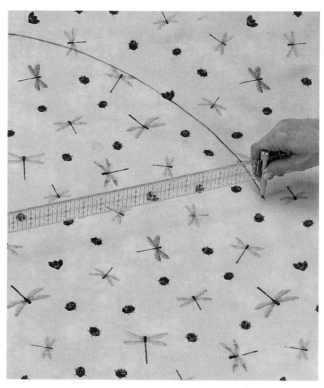

1 For a stool cover, trace the stool top onto tracing or freezer paper. Add a ½" seam allowance to the traced pattern.

2 For a pillow or tuffet top, place the fabric or a piece of paper on a surface that can be pinned into. Tie a piece of string around a sharp pencil or fabric marker. Measure the radius of the circle (half the diameter), plus ½" for a seam allowance onto the string and insert a pin through the string at this point. Insert the pin into the fabric or paper. With the pencil or marker held straight up and the string tight, draw a circle.

3 Use a pillow template with circular markings or an Omnigrid® yardstick and Dritz® Compass Points, following the manufacturer's instructions.

Cutting Perfect Pillow Corners

Knife-edge pillow corners that are cut square will appear floppy after the pillow form is inserted. To avoid this, use a tapered corner pillow template to mark the panels for cutting, or taper the corners after cutting out the pillow panels as follows:

1 Fold one pillow panel into fourths and mark the distance halfway between the corner and each folded edge.

2 Make a mark ½" from both corner edges. Draw a line to connect the marks.

3 Cut on the marked lines through all layers.

4 Repeat for the remaining panel.

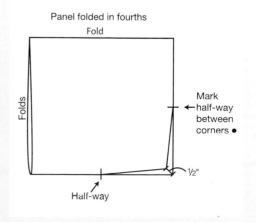

Panel folded in fourths

Fold

Folds

Mark
←half-way
between
corners ●

Half-way

½"

Sewing Basics

Seam Allowance

For most home décor sewing and for all projects in this book, sew seams with right sides together and use a ½" seam allowance unless otherwise indicated.

Sewing Corners

When sewing a boxing strip, separate flange, ruffle, or welting to pillow or cushion corners, it's necessary to clip the seam allowance so the layers will lie flat while you sew and appear smooth and flat when completed. Sew the layers together with the edges aligned and the band, flange, or ruffle on top.

If the fabric you're using ravels easily, staystitch just inside the seamline on the band, flange or ruffle areas that will be sewn around the corner or curve.

For outside curves, clip the upper layer seam allowance just enough to let it lie flat as you sew.

For outside corners:

1 Sew the seam to exactly ½" from the approaching edge and leave the needle down in the fabric.

2 Clip up close to, but not beyond the needle. If the band has a seam at the corner, clip the seamline stitching up to the needle; apply seam sealant after sewing to prevent the seam from separating.

3 Pivot the fabric, aligning the raw edges and continue sewing.

Edge Finishes

Welting

It's easy to make welting in the size you want by covering cotton filler cord with bias-cut fabric strips. Cotton filler cord is readily available by the yard in diameters ranging from ⁵⁄₃₂" to 1¾". Choose a size that's proportionate to the pillow or cushion you're making.

1 To determine the welting length you will need, loosely measure the edge or edges where it will be applied and add 3" for an overlap.

2 To determine the width of the bias strips you will need to cover the cording, measure around the cording and add 1" for seam allowances.

3 Cut the bias strips and cover the cording as follows.

Creating Continuous Bias Strips

I learned this clever and reliable technique of creating continuous bias strips when I was on the staff of *Sewing Décor* magazine almost a decade ago, and have used it ever since. It enables you to create a small or large quantity of straight, even strips in a fraction of the time it takes to cut and piece the strips using traditional methods.

This method begins with a perfect square of the fabric you're planning to use for the bias strips. To determine how many yards of strips per given fabric, use this formula: Multiply the square length times two; divide this number by the width of the strips to be cut, then divide again by 36". For example, to determine the number of 3"-wide bias strips a 30" fabric square will yield: 30" x 30"=900"; 900"÷3=300"; 300"÷36"=8.33"; the fabric square will yield 8⅓ yards of 3"-wide strips. Keeping this in mind, cut a perfect square in the size you've determined, then proceed as follows:

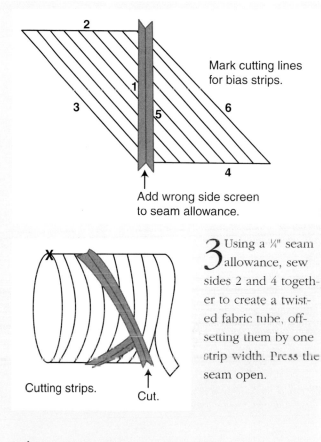

Mark cutting lines for bias strips.

Add wrong side screen to seam allowance.

Cutting strips. Cut.

3 Using a ¼" seam allowance, sew sides 2 and 4 together to create a twisted fabric tube, offsetting them by one strip width. Press the seam open.

4 Begin at the offset end and cut along the marked lines.

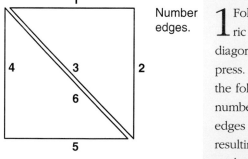

Number edges.

1 Fold the fabric on the diagonal and press. Cut along the fold line; number the edges of the resulting triangles as shown.

2 Sew edges 1 and 5 together using a ¼" seam allowance and press the seam open. Begin at one diagonal edge and use a clear ruler to mark lines in the desired strip width. Cut off any excess fabric after the last full-width strip.

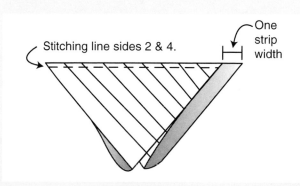

Stitching line sides 2 & 4.

One strip width

Covering Cording

1 Wrap the bias strip around the cording with wrong sides together and raw edges aligned.

2 Using a welting or zipper foot, baste the layers together ⅛" from the cord edge.

Applying Welting

To apply welting to the edge of pillow or cushion panels:

1 Beginning at the center of the lower or least conspicuous panel edge, pin or use basting tape to position the welting with the raw edges toward the outside and the basting line ⅛" inside the panel seam allowance.

2 At each corner, clip the welting flange close to, but not into the seamline. Pivot the corner and continue pinning in place.

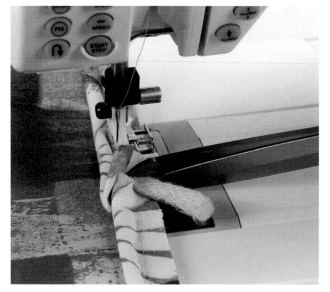

3 1" from the welting end, sew in place along the seamline to 2" from the opposite end. Leave the needle in the fabric and the presser foot down.

4 To join the welting ends, remove several basting stitches from the welting and open the fabric to reveal the cording. Cut the cording even with the beginning end, leaving the fabric intact.

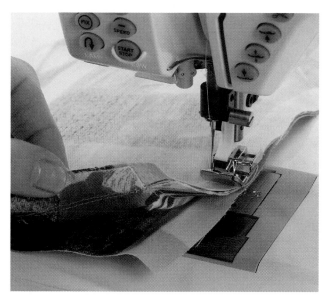

5 Trim the bias fabric to overlap the beginning end 1½". Turn the fabric end under ½" and wrap around the beginning end. Align the raw edges and pin in place. Continue sewing the overlap in place.

6 Pin the remaining panel in place, aligning edges and sandwiching the welting between the layers.

7 Use a cording or zipper foot and sew the layers together along the seamline, leaving an opening for turning. The stitching should be close to the cording, approximately ⅛" inside the basting line.

Trims without Lips

Trims without lips can be topstitched to the front pillow panel along the outside of the seam-

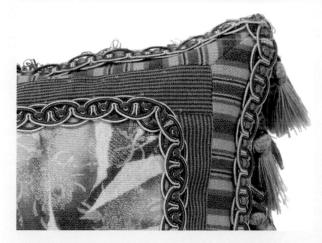

line before the pillow is assembled, or they can be slipstitched or adhered to the finished edge with permanent fabric adhesive.

You can also add a lip to the trim for insertion in the seam as follows:

1 Purchase twill tape, ribbon, or lightweight braid for the lip in the same length as the trim.

2 If the trim is very thick, whipstitch the lip edge to the trim.

3 For lighter weight or flat trims, align the lip edge with the trim edge. With the presser foot riding slightly over the trim edge, sew a long zigzag stitch along the lip edge, catching the trim in the stitching.

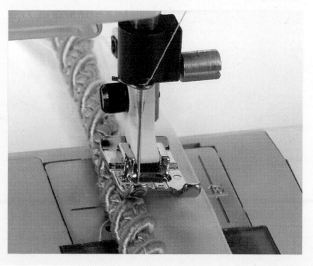

Applying Twisted Cord and Other Trims with a Lip

Twisted cord, fringe, and other trims with a lip are applied to the fabric edge in the same manner as welting. The only difference is the way the ends are finished. To finish the ends on twisted cord:

1 Stop sewing 1½" before the end. Clip the threads that secure the cord to the lip for 1½" at each cord end. Wrap tape around the individual cord ends to prevent raveling.

2 Overlap the lip ends and tape together. Twist each set of cord ends back to their original appearance. Overlap the ends of the two sets and tape to the lip; the cord should appear continuous.

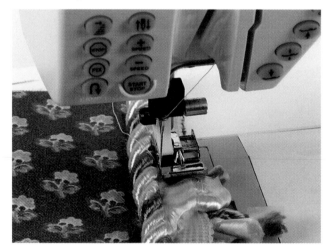

3 Sew in place along the seamline.

Flanges

A flange is a flat fabric extension beyond the body of the pillow. The inner edges of a flange can be stitched, secured with lacing through grommets, snaps, or buttons. It can be an extension of the panel or another fabric that is sewn onto the panel. Pillows made of leather, suede, fleece, or other non-fraying fabrics are perfect candidates for flanges that are cut to make self-fringe.

Several flange styles and instructions for making them are featured in the pillows chapter.

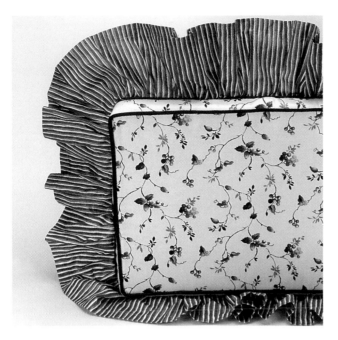

Ruffles

A ruffle can be gathered or pleated and made from a single or doubled layer of fabric in any fullness that pleases you. Generally, lighter fabric weights are doubled and fuller and heavier fabric weights are gathered less and used as a single layer. A good rule of thumb is to plan on cutting and piecing lightweight strips three times the length of the edge perimeter and medium- to heavyweight strips two to two and one-half times the perimeter length. Allow for ½" seam allowances on pieced strips.

To cut and piece the ruffle strips:

1 For a doubled ruffle, double the desired width and add 1" for seam allowances.

2 For a single ruffle, add 1" to the desired width for seam and hem allowances.

3 Sew the short ends together to make a long strip.

4 For a doubled ruffle, press the strip in half lengthwise with wrong sides together.

Ruffles can be made in several ways, including using a gathering or ruffler foot, by gathering the fabric with basting stitches or by zigzag stitching over cording. For light- to medium-weight fabrics, any of these techniques can be used. For heavy or bulky fabrics, zigzag stitching over cording works best.

Specialty Feet: Ruffles made with specialty feet aren't adjustable after they are stitched, so experiment with fabric scraps to determine how tight to make the gathers. Follow instructions given in your sewing machine manual to use the accessory feet.

Basting Stitches: The gathers on ruffles made with basting stitches are adjustable until they are sewn onto the panel. To gather a ruffle with basting stitches:

1 Sew two rows of basting stitches along the ruffle strip upper edge, sewing one row on the seamline and the second row ⅛" inch inside the seamline.

2 Pull the basting threads to gather the ruffle to the desired length and knot the thread ends together.

3 Evenly distribute the ruffles.

Stitching Over Cording: To gather heavy fabrics, use narrow cording for gathering as follows:

1 Use a zigzag or cording foot and set your machine for a wide, medium-length zigzag stitch.

2 Center the cording on the seam allowance and zigzag stitch over it, being careful not to catch the cording in the stitching.

3 Pin the cording to the fabric at one end. Pull the opposite end to gather the fabric to the desired fullness. Knot the cord ends together to secure.

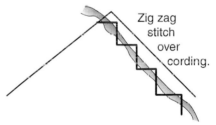

Zig zag stitch over cording.

Finishing

1 To make a continuous ruffle, sew the ruffle short ends together.

2 To hem a single layer ruffle, serge or finish the edge and press under ½". Topstitch ⅜" from the folded edge.

Attaching Ruffles

To attach the ruffle to the fabric panel:

1 With the raw edges aligned, pin the ruffle to the panel edge.

2 Sew in place.

Pleats

Both box pleats and knife pleats add a tailored touch to pillow or cushion ruffles or tuffet skirts. Box pleats have an inward fold on each side, while knife pleat folds are all facing the same direction. Knife pleats can also be made using a ruffler attachment on your sewing machine; consult your owner's manual to determine yardage and pleat width using a ruffler.

Pleats can be made in the width of your choice and require advance planning to calculate the appropriate number of whole pleats that will fit an edge. To figure the number of pleats and the length of the fabric strip:

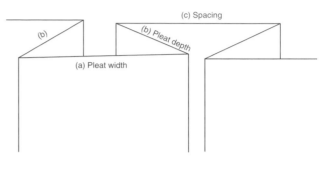

1 To calculate the number of pleats that will evenly along a panel edge, measure the perimeter of the panel. Divide the perimeter edge by the desired pleat width for side-by-side pleats and the combined pleat and spacing width for pleats with spacing between them; adjust the pleat width as needed until you calculate a whole number.

2 For box pleats, determine the width of the pleat (a), the depth of the side folds (b) and the spacing between the pleats, measuring from inside fold to inside fold (c). *Note:* The inward fold can measure up to half of the pleat width. Add these measurements together for each pleat and multiply by the determined number of pleats to calculate the cut length of the fabric strip to be pleated.

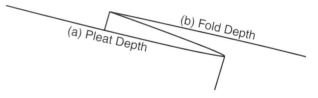

3 For knife pleats, determine the width of the pleat (a) and the depth of the fold (b); the depth of the fold can be up to half of the width of the pleat. Add these measurements together for each pleat and multiply by the determined number of pleats to calculate the cut length of the fabric strip to be pleated.

4 Cut the fabric strip to be pleated. Finish the lower edge with zigzag stitches or serging; turn up and topstitch a ½" hem. Mark the determined pleat and fold measurements on the upper edge.

5 Press the pleats at the marks and pin in place.

6 Baste across the upper edge of the pleats to secure.

7 Pin to the fabric panel with raw edges aligned and sew in place.

Prairie Points Strip

Popular with quilters, this edge finish adds a novel and decorative touch to pillows or cushions. Unlike the traditional technique of making individual points to sew together, this clever method of cutting and folding two continuous strips is both quick and easy. To make a strip of prairie points, each 3" wide and 2" deep with two fabric colors:

1 Measure the circumference of the edge where the strips will be applied. From each fabric color, cut a 4½"-wide crosswise strip or cut and piece strips equal to this length, plus 1" for seam allowances.

2 With right sides together, sew ½" from one long edge. Begin at the end of one strip and cut to the seam every 4". Turn the strip over. Beginning 2" from the same end on the second color, cut and continue cutting every 4".

3 Open the strip with the wrong side up. Fold each square in half diagonally to the stitching line with wrong sides together; all folds should face the same direction.

4 Fold each square in half again to the stitching line and pin in place.

5 Baste the upper edges in place.

Pillow and Cushion Closures

Pillow and cushion covers can be closed by the following methods of slipstitching, overlapping edges, or inserting zippers.

There are also a number of decorative techniques that can be used, such as lacing, button-on toppers, and ties that will be presented in the "Pillows" chapter of this book.

Slipstitching

The easiest closure to make for pillows or cushions is to press under the opening seam allowances and slipstitch the opening closed by hand. This is the least obvious method and is especially recommended for covers that won't

need to be removed for cleaning. Even if the cover does need to be removed, you can remove the slipstitching and stitch again after cleaning.

Overlapped Edges

The edges of an overlapped closure can simply overlap, or can be secured by Velcro™, buttons and buttonholes, snaps, or ties. To make an overlapped closure:

1 Determine the placement of the closure and the width of each finished section. For pillows, an overlapped closure can be in the center back, in the front, or off center on pillows for a decorative effect.

For a box-edge cushion, the back boxing strip is cut in two sections and overlapped. An overlap of 1½" is suitable for secured closures and smaller pillows styles, but you may want to make it up to 5" deep for large pillows or pillow shams. Each edge will require a 2" hem allowance, regardless of the overlap depth.

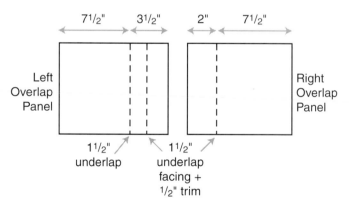

2 Using pattern tracing cloth or paper, draw a pattern for the pillow panel, adding a ½" seam allowance to each edge. Draw a line across the panel to indicate the edges that will overlap. Label the sections as the underlying panel or the overlapping panel and indicate the edges to be lapped. Cut out the pattern pieces, cutting along the overlap line.

3 To make a 1½" overlap, pin the pattern pieces, spaced 6" apart, on the wrong side of the fabric. Using a fabric marker and clear ruler, add a 2" hem allowance to each edge that will be lapped. Add an additional 1½" to the underlying panel.

4 Cut out the panels. To hem the overlapping edges, press ½", then 1½" to the wrong side; topstitch close to the inner fold.

5 If desired, add evenly space buttons and button-holes or snaps to the overlap.
For a Velcro closure, cut the strips 3" shorter than the overlapping edges. Center and sew the loop side strip to the right side of the underlying edge; sew the hook side strip to the wrong side of the overlapping edge.

6 Baste the ends of the overlapped edges together along the seamline, then complete the pillow or cushion assembly.

Zippers

Zippers provide an attractive and practical way to close pillow or cushion covers that you will want to remove for cleaning.

Knife Edge Pillows

Zippers can be hidden in a pillow side seam or placed across the back, providing both a practical and attractive method of closing a removable cover. Purchase a dressmaker's zipper that is approximately 2" shorter than the finished length of the opening.

1 Referring to the overlap instructions above, draw and cut a pattern for the panel sections that will be zipped together. Pin to the fabric edge, adding a 1" seam allowance to each zipper opening edge.

2 Pin the sections together along the zipper opening edges. Sew a 1½" seam at each end, then baste along the seamline between the stitched ends. Press the seam open and mark the ends of the basting.

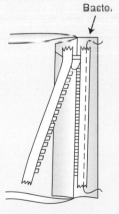

Basto.

3 With the panel wrong side up, extend one seam allowance. Open the zipper. Using basting tape, adhere one section right side down over the seam allowance basting, aligning the zipper teeth with the seamline. Machine-baste along the woven zipper tape guideline, stitching through the zipper tape and seam allowance only.

4 Close the zipper and turn it right side up with the seam allowance folded under. Press the fold close to the zipper teeth. Topstitch close to the fold through the zipper tape and seam allowance.

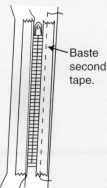

Baste second tape.

5 Open the panels flat with the zipper right side down. Adhere the remaining zipper tape in place with basting tape. Baste in place through all layers.

6 Turn the panel right side up and topstitch around the zipper. Remove the basting threads.

Box Edge Pillows and Cushions

For box edge pillows and cushions, zippers are inserted across the center of least conspicuous boxing strip edge—usually the back edge for seat cushions and the lower edge for chair back cushions or pillows.

The best zipper length depends on the intended use of the cushion. For a pillow or a cushion that will be viewed from three sides, use a zipper that is several inches shorter than the edge. If a cushion will be used in a chair or settee where the sides will be hidden, select a zipper that is 6" to 8" longer than the back edge of the cushion—the longer the zipper, the easier it is to remove a cushion cover. Use a dressmaker's zipper for pillows or cushions that are smaller and will be lightly used. Use an upholstery zipper for chair or settee cushions that are large or will be used frequently. Upholstery zippers are available in pre-cut lengths or by the yard.

1 To determine the width and length of the front and sides boxing strip, measure the cushion depth and add 1" for the strip width. For the length, measure the cushion perimeter and subtract the zipper length; add 1" for seam allowances.

2 For the zipper box strips, cut two strips equal to the zipper length. The width of each strip should be half of the cushion thickness, plus 1½" for seam allowances.

3 Baste the zipper box strips together along one long edge, using a 1" seam allowance. Press the seam open.

4 Center the zipper right side down over the seam allowance. Secure the edges with basting tape. Sew both zipper tapes in place.

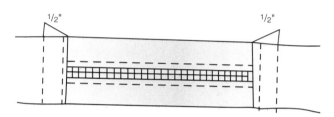

5 Press the ends of the front/sides boxing strip under ½".

6 Place each end over a zipper strip end and topstitch close to the fold. Stitch again to add stability.

Tufting

Tufting adds interest and dimension to pillows, cushions, and tuffets. Depending on the thickness of the project you are tufting, you'll need waxed button thread or sturdy yarn and a long upholstery needle. You'll also need buttons for both sides of most of the tufted projects in this book. For lightly stuffed pillows or cushions, such as the "Tufted Stool Cushion" on page 88, you can use thread or yarn only for tufting and ties.

Tufting Pillows with Buttons

To tuft pillows or cushions with buttons, you'll need two buttons for each tuft. To make each tuft:

1 Mark the placement of the tufts on each side of the pillow or cushion.

2 Cut an 18" length of waxed thread. For buttons with shanks, tie the center of the thread to the button shank. For buttons with two holes, insert the thread ends through the holes and pull until the button is centered; for buttons with four holes, cut two thread lengths, and insert the ends through opposite holes.

3 Thread the upholstery needle with one thread end and stitch through the pillow or cushion just to the right of the tufting mark, to the corresponding point on the opposite side. Repeat for the remaining thread end, stitching ⅛" to the left of the first stitch. For four threads, stitch the remaining threads through the pillow above and below the tuft mark.

4 Insert the thread ends through the shank or holes of a button on the opposite side. Pull the thread tightly to create the desired tufting depth, then knot the thread ends securely. For buttons with holes, insert the thread ends through the holes to the underside of the button and tie off. Cut the excess thread ends.

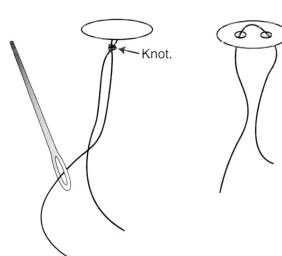

← Knot.

Tufting Pillows or Cushions with Yarn or Thread

You can tuft pillows and cushions that aren't too thick or densely filled with only yarn or heavy thread. To tuft with thread or yarn:

1 Thread the upholstery needle with at least two 12" thread strands or yarn plies.

2 At each tuft mark, insert the needle through the pillow and out at the corresponding point on the opposite side.

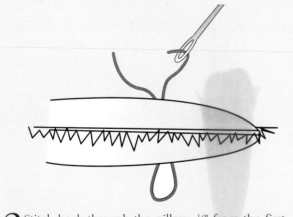

3 Stitch back through the pillow, ¼" from the first stitch.

4 Pull the thread or yarn ends to the desired tightness, then knot the ends together. Trim the ends ½" to 1" long.

Tufting Tuffets

Tufting through the thick, dense upholstery foam used for tuffets requires sturdy buttons and shanks. You will need one shank button and one flat metal button with holes for each tuft. You'll also need an electric drill to make holes in the wood and an ice pick to make holes in the foam.

If you experience difficulty with buttons or shanks breaking when you tighten the thread on very thick foam, try using small, flat metal buttons for the initial tufting. After tufting, sew a decorative button over the metal button, attaching it in the same manner as the tufting technique.

To tuft a tuffet:

1 Mark the placement for each tuft on the wood base before assembling the tuffet top. Use a drill with a ¼" bit to drill a hole at each mark.

2 Assemble the tuffet top following the project instructions.

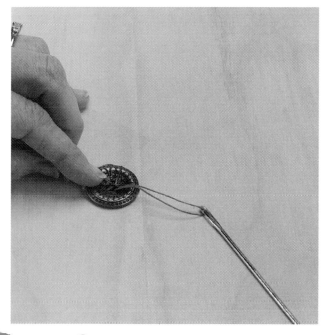 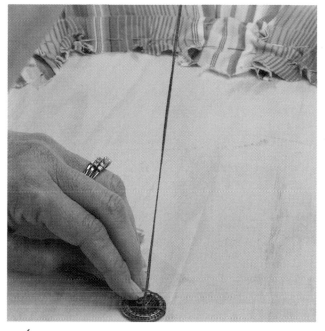

3 Mark tuft placements to correspond with the holes in the wood base on the fabric surface. Use an ice pick to make a hole through the fabric and foam at each mark.

4 Depending on the foam thickness, cut an 18" to 30" length of waxed thread for each tuft. Knot the center of the thread around the button shank and thread the upholstery needle with both ends. With the shank button on top, insert the needle through the hole in the fabric, foam, and wood base.

5 On the wood base side, insert the thread ends through a flat button with holes.

6 Tie in a slipknot to secure. Pull the threads tightly to create the desired tuft depth then knot the ends securely with a double knot.

CHAPTER 3

Creative Touches

This is what I love to do! It's so much fun to let your imagination run wild and take your home décor sewing one step further by adding your own decorative accents. From working with design elements like stripes and fabric patterns to embroidery and painted accents, a world of creative possibilities awaits you.

Best of all, you don't have to be an artist to embellish fabric or work with paint. Thanks to the array of easy-to-use products, techniques such as embellishing with crystals, stamping, and photo transferring are easier than ever. And that's just the beginning. So try some of these artistic expressions ... or put on your creative thinking cap and you'll be sure to think of many more of your own.

Working with Fabric Design

When is a fabric design more than just a pretty print or stripe? When you look past the obvious and view it for its creative potential as a surface to be embellished.

Stripe Sensations: A stripe may appear pretty basic when it's displayed on a fabric bolt. But miter it to form outside angles for squares or inside angles for V-shapes, or use it as a guide for making pleats, and it takes on a new life.

Mitered Stripes: The appearance of mitered stripes depends on the direction in which the pieces are cut. Stripes on fabric usually run along the lengthwise grain. Pieces cut on the lengthwise grain will result in outside angles when mitered together; pieces cut on the crosswise grain will result in inside angles when pieced together. All pieces to be mitered together must be cut identically.

To create a mitered panel:

1 On pattern tracing cloth or tracing paper, draw a square or circle equal to the desired finished panel size, plus 1" for seam allowances. Use a straight edge to divide it diagonally into four triangles. Add ½" seam allowances to the sides of one triangle and cut out to use as a pattern.

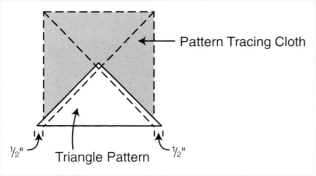

Pattern Tracing Cloth

½" ← Triangle Pattern → ½"

2 For stripes that form inside angles when pieced, place the pattern on the lengthwise grain and cut four identical pieces.

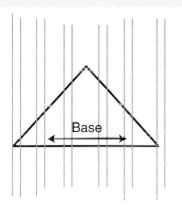

Base

For Inside Angles

3 For stripes that form outside angles when pieced, place the pattern on the crosswise grain and cut four identical pieces.

4 Sew the panels together, making sure the stripes match at the seamlines.

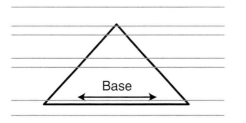

Base

For Outside Angles

Pleated Stripes: To use stripes as a guide for pleating:

1 Select a stripe fabric with stripes in a width you like for pleats.

2 Cut out the fabric to be pleated and mark the pleats along the edge, using the stripes as a guide.

3 Press the pleats in place along the stripe edges and baste across the upper edge.

Quilted Dimensions

Any fabric with medium-to-large, well-defined motifs is a perfect candidate for outline quilting. Depending on the thickness of the batting and the thread color used for stitching, the effect can vary from subtle to eye-catching. In addition to the decorative fabric, you will need fusible batting and muslin. To outline quilt:

1 Cut the decorative fabric, batting, and muslin to the desired panel size. Fuse the batting between the wrong sides of the fabrics, aligning edges.

2 Beginning in the center of the panel, pin the fabric layers together around the first motif to be outline quilted to avoid shifting. Stitch around the motif, close to the edge.

3 Remove the pins and repeat to stitch around the next motif, working from the center out.

Bedecked and Bejeweled

Ribbon, decorative trim, buttons, heat-applied crystals, and yarn tufts are ideal for fabric embellishments. You can sew the edges of almost any flat ribbon or trim along fabric motif outlines.

Couching—sewing over the surface of a decorative ribbon, cord or yarn by hand or machine—enables you to apply yarns, thicker cords, and decorative threads to the surface, or to create interesting effects with ribbon (see "Place Mat Pillows" on page 81 and "Couching," page 38).

Yarn or thread tufts, buttons, beads and heat-applied crystals also can be used to highlight design details such as the design line intersections on the palm tree pillow and the leopard eyes and flower petals on the tapestry pillow.

On the Surface: Creating Your Own Fabric Panels and Designs

Photo by Kevin May.

Feeling artistic? Why not create your own fabric panels or add decorative accents to the fabric of your choice? You can use any of the techniques mentioned above as well as techniques such as photo transfer, machine embroidery, couched and novelty trims, stamping, stenciling, and fabric paint.

Photo and Image Transfer

Turn favorite photos into pillow panels, create appliqués from photos or scan and print flat objects like postcards, greeting cards, pressed flowers or leaves onto fabric for use as panels. With today's selection of transfer products, these techniques are easy and fun. Look for printer fabric sheets that you print onto then use as fabric, and iron-on stabilizers for ink jet printers that enable you to stabilize the fabric of your choice for photo or image transfer.

Always follow the manufacturer's instructions for the printer sheets or stabilizer you've purchased. If you need assistance in storing photos onto a CD-ROM or floppy disk, photo shops, copy centers, and office sup-

ply stores often offer this service.

Generally, the photo transfer technique works as follows:

1 To use a color ink jet copier, place the printer fabric sheet in the paper tray so the printing will be on the fabric side. Place photos or flat objects in the copier and copy.

2 To use a color ink jet printer, use one of the following methods to obtain the image: Scan with a computer scanner, store your photos on a CD-ROM or floppy disk and import to a document, or use a digital camera and import to a document.

3 Place the printer fabric sheet in the paper tray and print on the fabric side. Let the ink dry, then remove the paper backing from the fabric. Follow the manufacturer's instructions for heat setting or a colorfast treatment.

4 To use iron-on stabilizer for printers, pre-treat the fabric of your choice with an ink jet ink-setting agent, found at fabric stores. Cut the fabric into pieces the size of the stabilizer sheets and iron in place, following the manufacturer's instructions.

5 Print, using one of the above techniques.

Machine Embroidery

Use machine embroidery or decorative stitches to embellish fabric panels for pillows or to create an overall design for a vanity bench cover.

Couching

Topstitch or couch trims to the fabric surface to create the designs of your choice. (See "Couched Fall Leaves Pillow" on page 75.)

Trim can be couched by hand sewing across the trim surface to adhere it in place or stitched with a sewing machine. The easiest method is to use a cording foot, but you can also couch many trims with a wide zigzag stitch. To machine couch trim:

1 Use a fabric marker to draw a line where the trim will be applied.

2 For a zigzag foot, set a medium stitch length and a stitch width wide enough to span the trim width without catching it in the stitching. Working with short lengths at a time, apply the trim to the line and stitch across it to secure.

3 For a cording foot, set the stitch width and length according to your machine manual. Feed the trim into the foot as you stitch along the line.

Faux Chenille Strips

Creating faux chenille strips with Chenille By The Inch™ from Fabric Café™ is a fun technique that adds dimension and a touch of nostalgia to your sewing. You can create the design of your choice or outline appliqués with this trim. It's available in sheets of pre-stitched fabric layers in a myriad of colors. You'll also need a Cutting Guide and Chenille Brush.

To use Chenille By The Inch:

1 Remove the tear-away stabilizer from the back of the fabric.

2 Using the cutting guide and a rotary cutter, cut the strips apart in the center between the stitching lines.

3 For fabrics with naps or types that snag, place a piece of tear-away stabilizer on the fabric before applying the Chenille By The Inch. Remove after brushing the chenille strips.

4 Sew the strips in place, overlapping the ends ¼" to begin or end strips or make circles.

5 Spray the strips lightly with water to soften the fibers. Using the entire surface of the chenille brush, brush back and forth in the direction of the strip to fray the fabric to the stitching line.

Stamping

Walk through any craft store or peruse the Internet and you'll be sure to find a stamp for almost any motif or design you can think of. My favorite stamps for fabric are Pelle's See Thru Stamps™ that allow you to see exactly where you're stamping the design. You can use any stamp as long as the design is well defined and not too detailed—small details tend to get lost in the fabric texture.

Be sure to use textile paint or ink designed for use on fabric and a clean textile inkpad or brayer to apply the paint. Regular acrylic paint will be stiff when dry and may crack or peel off over time.

To stamp using textile paint and an ink pad:

1 Pour a small amount of textile paint onto the inkpad. Use the back of a spoon to work it in until the pad is saturated.

2 Working on a hard surface, lightly tap the stamp up and down on the pad until the image is covered, but not saturated. Holding the stamp by the edges, press straight down on the fabric, pushing the stamp evenly with the fingers of your other hand. Lift the stamp straight up.

3 Repeat to stamp as many images as desired, cleaning the stamp if paint begins to pool in the cutout areas. Clean the stamp with mild soap and a toothbrush immediately after use.

4 Let the stamped images dry for 24 to 48 hours. Heat-set by ironing over each image for 30 to 45 seconds with the hottest setting the fabric will tolerate.

Decoratively Cut Edges

Because real or faux leather and suede do not ravel, it isn't necessary to hem the edges of these fabrics. You can simply leave them as cut edges or use a rotary cutter with a decorative blade to cut.

Coordinating Fabric and Painted Furniture

Photo by Kevin May, courtesy of *Creative Machine Embroidery* magazine.

Painted furniture and fabrics make perfect partners. Whether you begin with the painted piece and find coordinating fabric, or find a fabric you love then paint the furniture, you still achieve the same made-for-each-other effect.

Depending on your interest in painting and skill level, you can keep your designs basic or replicate the fabric design. Basic designs are easy to achieve when you paint dots, checks, and lines in colors to match the fabric. Or, if you enjoy painting floral or other motifs, as shown on the chair and bench, simply trace the fabric motifs of your choice onto tracing paper and transfer to the wood surface. Study the motif or refer to decorative painting books to paint the design. Acrylic paints are easiest to use, and several coats of a compatible varnish or polyurethane coating will ensure durability.

CHAPTER 4

Pillows

Pillows, pillows, everywhere—what else could add this much comfort to your decor? And best of all, they are the perfect decorating accent. For a minimal investment of money and time, you can accent any room with a bevy of plush pillows in varying shapes, sizes, and fabrics. Any sofa or chair becomes more comfortable and inviting with the addition of pillows, beds look luxurious when piled high with mix-and-match pillows that coordinate with the bedcover, and even the floor beckons you to sit down when a comfy pillow awaits.

While the possibilities for making pillows are
endless, all pillows are a variation of two shapes:
knife-edge and box-edge. A knife-edge pillow is
thicker in the center and tapers to the edges, with
very little or no side edge. A box-edge pillow is
the same thickness throughout and has a side
boxing strip. The long, round bolster pillow is
actually a box-edge pillow.

The finished size and materials to make that
size are given for each pillow in this chapter, but
you can easily make any of them in the size of
your choice—just be sure to adjust the materials
needed accordingly. Refer to Chapter 2 for all
general techniques.

Basic Knife Edge Pillows

Materials:
- Square pillow form
- Fabric in yardage for two panels and closure of choice
- Trim equal to perimeter of pillow, plus 2"
- Covered buttons for center tuft (optional)

Instructions:

1 For each pillow: Cut two panels with or without tapered corners, each 1" larger than the pillow form for a slipstitched closure. Refer to Chapter 2 (page 26) to cut panels for other closures.

2 Baste trim to the front panel edges. Sew the panels together, leaving an opening for turning.

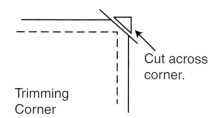

Cut across corner.

Trimming Corner

3 Trim the seam allowance across corners.

4 Turn right side out. Press the edges, pressing under the opening seam allowances. Insert the pillow form and slipstitch the opening closed.

5 Tuft the center with a button on each side, if desired.

Stripe Illusions Trio

Finished sizes: 16" and 18" square

Materials:
- 12" and 18" square pillow forms
- Stripe decorator fabric in determined yardage

Trims:
- Two 1½" covered buttons for each 18" pillow
- Two 3" tassels for the 12" pillow
- Waxed button thread
- 6" upholstery needle

Instructions:

1. Refer to "Mitered Stripes" on page 35 to create a triangle pattern and cut the panels.

    For each pillow, the yardage needed depends on the stripe width and how far apart the panels must be cut to achieve matching panels. Refer to "Mitered Stripes" on page 35 to make a template for each pillow size. Position the template on the fabric and determine the yardage you'll need for eight identical triangles.

2. For each 18" pillow with inside corner stripes, cut eight identical triangles with the template positioned on the crosswise grain. Position the template center over the stripe color you'd like to feature as the center crisscross design.

3. For the 12" pillow with outside corner stripes, cut eight identical triangles with the template positioned on the lengthwise grain.

4. Sew together two sets of four triangles each, matching the stripes at the seamlines.

5. Matching the stripes, sew the front and back panels together. Leave an opening for turning. Trim the corners, turn right side out and press.

6. On each 12" panel, clip the stitching at the panel center. Insert a tassel-hanging loop to ½" from the tassel top. Slipstitch the opening closed, securing the hanging loop.

7. Insert the pillow form and slipstitch the opening closed.

8. For each 18" pillow, cover two buttons with fabric. Tuft the pillow center with a button on each side. For the 12" pillow, tuft the center with thread only.

Trim Transformation

Finished size: 16" square

This paisley print pillow went from plain and unassuming to eye-catching in a matter of minutes, thanks to these unique trims. Fun-loving ostrich fringe accents the outer edges, while handmade raku buttons and beads add an artistic touch to the center.

Materials:

- 16" square pillow form
- ½ yd. of decorator fabric
- 2½" raku ginko leaf button
- Coordinating 1" button for tuft back
- Two 6" raku bead strings
- 2 yd. of ostrich fringe
- Permanent fabric adhesive
- Waxed button thread
- 6" upholstery needle

Instructions:

1 Follow the basic knife-edge pillow instructions to make the pillow.

2 Using waxed button thread, tie the top of the bead strings to the shank of the ginko leaf button, positioning the top of the beads at the edge of the button.

3 Tuft the pillow center using the raku button with beads on the front and the 1" button on the back.

4 Beginning and ending at the center of the lower edge, glue the fringe around the pillow. Cut a small length from the excess trim; glue to the pillow behind the button's upper edge.

Looped Corners

Finished size: 12" square

Materials:

- 12" square pillow form
- ½ yd. of decorator fabric
- 2½ yd. of twisted cord with lip
- Self-adhesive, double-sided basting tape
- Permanent fabric adhesive

Another quick fix, the looped trim on this pillow's corners makes it stand out from its plain-pillow counterparts. Easy to create with any twisted cord with a lip, you can make the corner design range from single to multiple loops.

Instructions:

1 From the decorator fabric, cut two 13"-square panels without tapered corners.

2 Beginning in the center of the front panel lower edge, use the basting tape to apply the trim lip to ½" from the corner. Cut the lip to the cord then carefully cut the lip away from the cord to create a 9" length of cord without a lip.

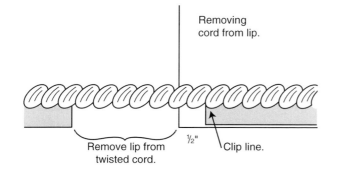

Removing cord from lip.

Remove lip from twisted cord.   ½"   Clip line.

3 Loop the cord without the lip toward the center of the panel. Resume adhering the lip to the pillow edge ½" from the corner to the next corner. Repeat Step 2 for each corner.

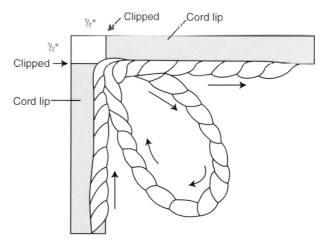

⅛"   Clipped   Cord lip

½"

Clipped →

Cord lip →

4 With the loops toward the panel center, sew the front and back panels together, leaving an opening for turning. Trim the corners, turn right side out and press. Insert the pillow form and slipstitch the opening closed.

5 Referring to the photo, fold each loop down and slipstitch to the pillow corner.

Tufted Flowers

Finished sizes: 14" and 18" diameters

Materials:

- 14" and 18" round pillow forms
- ½ yd. silk dupioni or embroidered silk brocade for 14" pillow
- ⅝ yd. silk dupioni or embroidered silk brocade for 18" pillow
- 3 yd. of ⅛"-wide satin ribbon for each pillow
- Two covered button forms for each pillow
- Waxed button thread
- Upholstery needle

It's easy to give a basic round pillow a flower shape when you wrap it with ribbon ties and tuft the center.

Instructions:

1 From the silk fabric, cut two circular panels 1" larger in diameter than the pillow form to be covered.

2 Sew the panels together, leaving an opening for turning. Turn right side out and press. Insert the pillow form and slipstitch the opening closed.

3 To create the petals, thread the upholstery needle with the ribbon and knot one ribbon end. Stitch through the center of the pillow, wrap the ribbon over the edge and stitch back through the center, pulling the ribbon taut. Repeat to stitch five more evenly spaced ribbon wraps around the pillow, then knot the ribbon securely in the center.

4 Follow the manufacturer's instructions to cover the buttons. Tuft the pillow center with a button on each side.

Tie-on Heirloom Handkerchief

Finished size: 16" square

Materials:

- 16" square pillow form
- ½ yd. of decorator fabric
- 12" to 13" handkerchief
- 2 yd. of ⅛"-wide ribbon
- Four ½" shell buttons
- Permanent fabric adhesive or hand sewing needle and thread
- Fabric marker

Instead of tucking Grandma's handkerchiefs away in a drawer, why not display them on pillows? By carefully tacking ribbon lengths to the corners, then tying them onto buttons, even fragile heirloom linens can be used without damaging them.

Instructions:

1 From the decorator fabric, cut two 17"-square panels with tapered corners.

2 Follow the "Basic Knife Edge Pillows" instructions on page 44 to sew and turn the panels.

3 Cut the ribbon into four 18" lengths. Use fabric adhesive or a needle and thread to tack the center of each ribbon length to the wrong side of a handkerchief corner.

4 Center the handkerchief on the front pillow panel. Mark each button placement ½" from a corner. Sew the buttons in place. Tie each ribbon length into a bow around a button.

5 Insert the pillow form and slipstitch the opening closed.

Panel Play

Showcase a favorite fabric print, needle-work design, or photo transfer when you give it center stage on a pillow front. From quick-fuse techniques to pieced panels and borders, the following pillows are fun to make and afford endless possibilities for combining fabrics and trims. For round or diamond-shape panels, it's easiest to fuse or sew the center panel to a full-size background panel. Square or rectangu-lar center panels can also be applied to a back-ground panel, but are easily pieced into the panel.

Using pillow templates (see page 13) is especially helpful for making pillows with cen-ter panels, as the clear template allows you to easily center the motif before marking the panel outline.

Toile Circle Panel

Finished size: 18" square

Materials:

- Square pillow form
- ⅝ yd. of plaid
- ½ yd. of toile
- 2¼ yd. of twisted cord with lip
- 1½ yd. of tassel fringe
- Iron-on adhesive sheet
- Permanent fabric adhesive

Toile fabric tells a story of its own, and usually offers multiple motifs that are perfect for "framing" as center panels. This center panel is fused in place before trimming, making it a quick and easy embellishment for the basic corded-edge pillow.

Instructions:

1 From the plaid fabric, cut two 19" squares with tapered corners for the pillow front and back panels. From the toile fabric, cut a 14" circle with a centered motif. Also cut a 14" circle of iron-on adhesive.

2 Follow the manufacturer's instructions to fuse the adhesive to the wrong side of the toile circle. Remove the paper backing and fuse the toile circle to the center of the front pillow panel. Apply cording to the edge, joining the ends in the center of the lower edge.

3 Sew the panels together, leaving an opening for turning. Clip the corners, turn right side out and press.

4 Begin at the bottom of the toile circle and use permanent fabric adhesive to glue the trim to the circle, covering the raw edge. Turn under and overlap the end, then glue in place. Let the adhesive dry.

5 Insert the pillow form and slipstitch the opening closed.

On-point Floral Panel

Finished sizes: 18" and 14" square

Materials:

- 14" square pillow form
- ½ yd. of textured solid
- ⅓ yd. of floral print
- 1 yard of beaded trim
- 1¾ yd. of flat trim for center panel
- 1¾ yd. of novelty brush fringe
- Self-adhesive, double-sided basting tape
- Iron-on adhesive sheet (optional)

Give a square pillow a designer look with an on-point floral panel. It's easy when you fuse or sew the center panel to a full-size background panel and embellish the edges with beaded and flat trim. For even more interest, cut and sew border strips to the center panel before applying it to the background, as shown in the Tropical Vase Pillow (see credits and "Pieced Border Panel" on page 53).

Instructions:

1 From the textured solid fabric, cut two 15" panels with tapered corners for the pillow front and back. From the floral fabric, cut a 12" square positioned on-point, with a centered floral motif.

2 Center and sew or fuse the on-point floral panel to the front pillow panel.

3 Using basting tape along the flat trim upper edge, apply it to the center panel edges, crisscrossing at the points. Cut a beaded trim length to fit each flat trim lower edge. Use basting tape to adhere the beaded trim header to the wrong side of the flat trim lower edge.

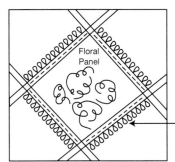

Beaded trim header applied to wrong side of trim.

4 Use a zipper foot and stitch along both edges of each flat trim length.

5 Apply brush fringe to the front panel edges, overlapping the ends in the center of the lower edge.

6 Sew the panels together, leaving an opening for turning. Trim the corners, turn right side out and press. Insert the pillow form and slipstitch closed.

Pieced Border Floral Panel

Finished size: 16" square

Materials:

- 16"-square pillow form
- ½ yd. each of floral motif for center panel and coordinating multi-color stripe for outer border and back
- ¼ yd. of tone-on-tone stripe for inner border
- 1½ yd. of flat trim
- 2 yd. of flat trim with tassels
- Self-adhesive, double-sided basting tape

There's no limit to how large you can make a center panel pillow when you add borders to the center panel. Make them narrow or wide, the same, or varying sizes and with or without trims.

You're limited only by your imagination. The Floral Panel Pillow features narrow borders, while the Monkey Pillow (see Credits) features the same size center panel with wider borders and an additional row of trim.

Instructions:

1 From the floral motif fabric, cut one 12" square, centering the desired motif. From the inner border stripe, cut four 2" x 13" strips. From the outer border/backing stripe, cut four 2½" x 17" strips with the stripes identically placed for the outer border and one 17" square for the back.

2 To add the inner border strips, with right sides together and raw edges even, align the end of one inner border strip with a center panel edge. Sew the long edges and press the strip open. Align the adjacent

border strip width as shown and sew in place. Press open.

Sewing Second Border Strip

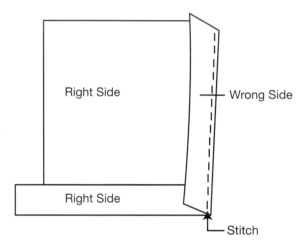

Repeat to add the two remaining strips. Sew the end of the final strip to the edge of the first strip to complete the border.

Sewing Final Strip

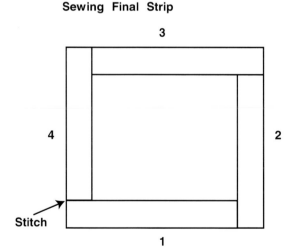

3 Center an outer border strip on each edge of the inner border with raw edges even. To miter the corners, sew the strips to the panel, beginning and ending ½" from each corner. Align and pin the raw edges of two adjacent border strips and fold the panel diagonally. Mark a line across the strips at a 45-degree angle, beginning at the end of the previous stitching line. Sew on the marked line.

Mitering Strips

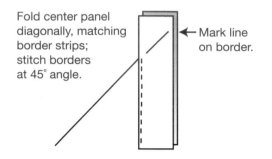

Repeat for each corner. Trim the seam allowances and press open.

4 Sew the back panel to the pieced front, leaving an opening for turning. Trim the corners, turn right side out and press.

5 Use permanent fabric adhesive to glue flat trim around the center panel edge, beginning and ending at the center of the lower edge. Turn the end under and glue; trim excess trim. Overlap the beginning end and glue in place. Repeat to glue the tasseled flat trim around the outer edges of the front panel. Let the glue dry.

6 Insert the pillow form and slipstitch the opening closed.

Mix and Match Panels

Part of the fun of decorating is mixing and matching fabrics to create an inviting ensemble such as the duvet cover, pillow shams, and pillows shown on page 41. Thanks to coordinating fabric collections, the selection process is easy— just choose three to five of your favorite prints, plaids, stripes, or checks. Use one or two as your main fabrics for a duvet cover and dust ruffle, then mix them with the other fabrics for the remaining projects. These pillows feature different motifs from the same fabric for the center, and the same stripe fabric applied differently for a coordinated, but not matching effect.

Fringe Framed Panels

Finished size: 14" x 18"

Materials:

- 14" x 18" pillow form
- ½ yd. of floral motif for center panel and back
- ¼ yd. each of stripe and check fabrics
- 1⅛ yd. of narrow twisted cord with lip
- 1½ yd. of tassel fringe
- 2 yd. of loop fringe with decorative header
- Self-adhesive, double-sided basting tape
- Permanent fabric adhesive

Instructions:

1 From the floral fabric, cut one 15" x 19" rectangle for the back and one 8" x 10" horizontal panel for the center front. From the stripe fabric, cut two 5½" x 8" side strips with the stripes running horizontally. From the check fabric, cut two 4½" x 19" upper and lower border strips.

2 Sew the side strips to the center panel sides and press open. Sew tassel fringe over the seamline, cutting the trim ends even with the fabric panel.

3 Use basting tape to apply the narrow cord with lip along the upper and lower edges of the pieced panel. Sew the border strips to the upper and lower edges. Press open.

4 Sew tassel fringe to the upper and lower borders next to the twisted cord.

5 Sew the back panel to the front pieced panel, leaving an opening for turning. Trim the corners, turn right side out and press.

6 With the loops to the outside and half of the header depth extending beyond the panel edge, glue the loop fringe to the front pillow panel edge. Let the glue dry.

7 Insert the pillow form and slipstitch the opening closed.

Shirred Pieced Panels

Finished size: 12" x 16"

Materials:

- 12" x 16" pillow form
- ½ yd. of floral motif for center panel, outer side borders and back
- ⅔ yd. of striped fabric
- 1⅓ yd. of loop fringe with decorative header
- 2¾ yd. of shirring tape
- Permanent fabric adhesive

Instructions:

1 From the floral fabric, cut one 13" x 9" vertical rectangle for the center panel, one 13" x 17" rectangle for the back and two 13" x 2" strips for the outer side borders. From the striped fabric, cut two 24" x 4" strips with the stripe running lengthwise for the shirred side borders. Cut the shirring tape into four 24" lengths.

2 On the wrong side of each striped strip, sew shirring tape along each long edge. To sew the tape in place, make certain the tape gathers will be aligned when pulled, and stitch close to both long edges. Pull the cords to evenly shirr the fabric to 13". Baste the long edges to secure the shirring.

3 Sew the shirred side strips to the center panel sides and press open. Sew the outer border strips to the remaining shirred panel edges and press open.

4 Sew the back panel to the front pieced panel, leaving an opening for turning. Trim the corners, turn right side out and press.

5 With the loops to the outside and half of the header depth extending beyond the panel edge, glue the loop fringe to the front pillow panel edge. Let the glue dry.

6 Insert the pillow form and slipstitch the opening closed.

Pieced Bolster

Finished size: 34" long

Materials:

- 20"-long bolster pillow form (19" circumference)
- ½ yd. of check for ends
- ⅓ yd. of floral motif for center panel
- ¼ yd. of stripe for side strips
- 2¼ yd. of brush fringe
- 1¼ yd. of ½" cord with lip
- Two chair ties
- Self-adhesive, double-sided basting tape

A bolster pillow adds another shape to a collection of pillows. The cover is made as a pieced rectangular panel with the long edges sewn together, and hemmed ends tied with chair ties provide an easy closure option. To make a cover for any bolster pillow form size, measure the form circumference and add 1" for seam allowances to determine the necessary panel height.

Instructions:

1 From the check, cut two 20" x 15" strips for the ends. From the floral motif, cut one 20" x 9" center panel. From the stripe, cut two 20" x 3-1/2" side strips.

2 Use basting tape to adhere the cord with lip to the long edges of the floral panel. Sew the side strips to the corded edges.

3 Cut four 20" brush fringe lengths. Use basting tape to adhere the headers to make two 20" lengths with double thickness. Baste to the remaining long-side strip edges.

4 For each end strip, serge or zigzag stitch one long edge. Press the finished edge under 4" and top-stitch in place. Sew the unfinished edge to the side strip.

5 Sew the pieced-panel long edges together. Turn right side out and insert the pillow form. With the form centered in the cover, tie the ends closed using chair ties.

Framed Photo Transfer Panel

Finished size: 14" x 16"

Portrait by Delayne Spain.

Materials:

- 14" x 16" rectangular pillow form
- ½ yd. of silk dupioni fabric
- 1½ yd. of 2¼"-wide woven trim
- 1 yd. each of matching loop fringe with decorative header and tasseled loop fringe with decorative header
- 7" x 9" photo to transfer
- Photo transfer paper
- ½ yd. of lightweight fusible interfacing
- Permanent fabric adhesive
- Self-adhesive, double-sided basting tape

We frame favorite photos to display on tables or walls, so why not frame a photo transferred to fabric for a pillow? It's easy when you use a wide woven trim with mitered corners to create a frame for the center photo panel. Silk dupioni fabric adds a luxurious texture to the pillow without distracting from the photo.

Mitered Trim Corner

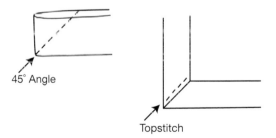

45° Angle

Topstitch

Instructions:

1. Follow the manufacturer's instructions for photo transfer paper to transfer the photo. Trim the fabric to 1" beyond the photo edges.

2. From both the silk dupioni and fusible interfacing, cut two 15" x 17" rectangles for the pillow panels. Fuse the interfacing to the wrong side of the silk.

3. Use basting tape to adhere the edges of the photo transfer to the center of one pillow panel.

4. Beginning at a corner and overlapping the photo edge, use basting tape to apply the woven trim around the photo, mitering the corners. To miter each corner, apply the trim to the corner, fold it back on itself and mark a 45-degree angle from the outside corner. Press the top strip up on the marked line and topstitch in place close to the folded edge.

5. To end, apply trim to the beginning corner, press the end under at a 45-degree angle and topstitch to the beginning end. Topstitch the trim close to each edge.

6. Sew the pillow panels together, leaving an opening for turning. Trim the corners and turn right side out.

7. With the loops facing out, glue the looped trim header to the upper and lower edges of the front panel. Glue the tasseled trim to the side edges, turning under and gluing the ends.

8. Insert the pillow form and slipstitch the opening closed.

Ribbon Bordered Needlepoint

Finished size: 12" square

Materials:

- 12"-square pillow form
- Blocked needlework with 9" design area
- ⅝ yd. of decorator fabric for back
- 1½ yd. 2"-wide grosgrain ribbon
- 1½ yd. tasseled loop fringe with decorative header
- 1¼ yd. of ½"-wide cord with lip
- 12" dressmaker's zipper

This design is a standard pillow form size, but you can finish any size needlework into a pillow with trim and a ribbon border. Cut the back fabric to fit the front, adding a zipper if desired. Make your own custom-size inset by sewing together cotton panels and stuffing with fiberfill to complete your pillow.

Instructions:

1 Refer to General Techniques page 26 to cut and assemble a 12½"-square back panel with a zipper 1" from the lower edge.

2 Mark a 9"-square outline around the needlework; trim the edges ½" beyond the marked line. Baste cord with lip around the edges.

3 Sew a ribbon border around the needlework, using a ¼" seam allowance and mitering the corners (see illustration on page 59). Press flat.

4 With the tassels toward the center and using a ¼" seam allowance, baste the tasseled trim header to the ribbon edge, basting tape to apply the woven trim around the photo, mitering the corners.

5 Sew the front and back panels together, using a ¼" seam allowance. Insert the pillow form through the zipper opening.

Decorative Edges and Flaps

Decorative edges, flaps, and flanges add new dimensions to basic pillow shapes and, like pieced panels, there's an endless number of ways you can vary the techniques. Consider the fabrics and trims you'd like to use then select a style that showcases them to their full potential.

Banded Button Closure

Finished size: 16" x 19"

Materials:

- 16"-square pillow form
- ½ yd. of floral print
- ¼ yd. of stripe
- 1 yd. of gimp
- Four buttons

This basic pillow dresses up when you add a contrasting buttoned band to an edge. While this band actually buttons, you can also capture the look without making buttonholes by sewing the band edges together and sewing on buttons. Eye-catching buttons like these shell butterflies add a special accent to either band option.

Instructions:

1. From the floral print, cut two 17"-square panels. From the stripe, cut one 7" x 33" strip for the band.

2. Sew the upper edges of the panels together and press the seam open. Sew the band strip to the side edge of the stitched panels. Serge or finish the band along the raw edge with zigzag stitches.

3. With the panels right sides together, sew the remaining side seam and the lower edge.

4. Press 3½" of the band to the inside and pin. Sew along the panel/band seamline to secure the band edge. Sew gimp over the seamline, overlapping the ends at the lower edge.

5. Evenly space and stitch four buttonholes on the band front. Sew corresponding buttons to the inside of the band back.

6. Insert the pillow form and button closed.

Band sewn to panels.

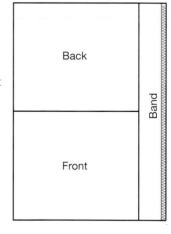

Button-on Reversible Topper

Finished size: 16" square

Materials:

- 16" square pillow form
- ½ yd. each of two silk dupioni colors and decorator print
- Fusible lightweight interfacing
- Six 1" buttons
- Fabric marker and clear ruler
- Tracing paper

Instructions:

1 For the pillow panels, cut two 17" x 16½" rectangles each from the dupioni, decorator print, and fusible interfacing. For the topper, cut one 17" x 15" rectangle each from the contrasting dupioni, decorator print and interfacing.

2 Fuse the interfacing pieces to the wrong side of the dupioni pieces. Trace the pattern on pages 122-123. Use the fabric marker and straight edge to draw the decorative edge design on the 15" edges of each topper piece and cut out.

3 To make the lined pillow panels, sew the dupioni panels right sides together along both 16½" side edges and the 17" lower edge. Repeat for the decorator print lining, leaving a 4" opening in the lower edge.

4 With right sides together and the raw upper edges aligned, place the dupioni panels inside the lining panels. Sew the upper edges together; turn right side out through the opening in the lining's lower edge. Slipstitch the opening closed. Turn the lining inside the dupioni panels, press and topstitch close to the edge. Insert the pillow form.

5 To make the topper, sew the dupioni and decorator print pieces together, leaving an opening in one side edge for turning. Trim the outside corners and clip the inside corners. Turn, press, and slipstitch the opening closed.

6 Stitch the buttonholes on the topper. Evenly wrap the topper over the top of the pillow form; mark each button placement on the pillow panels. Sew the buttons in place and attach the topper.

Reversible Envelope Flap

Finished size: 18" square

Materials:

- 18"-square pillow form
- ⅜ yd. of floral print
- ⅓ yd. each of coordinating textured solid and check for flap
- 2 yd. of ½" twisted cord with lip
- 4" tassel
- Medium-weight fusible interfacing
- Pattern tracing cloth
- Yardstick or long quilter's ruler
- Seam sealant

Envelope pillows can be made in several ways: The envelope flap can be a faced continuation of the back panel, a separate flap of a coordinating fabric or a separate flap with a different fabric on each side. This pillow features the last technique, giving the pillow a different look on each side when the flap is folded in that direction. For even more versatility, you could cut the pillow front and back panels from different coordinating fabrics.

Instructions:

1 From the floral print, cut two 19"-square panels. To make a pattern for the flap, use a yardstick or long quilter's ruler to draw a triangle with a 19" base and 10½" height to the tip; add a ½" seam allowance to the base edge.

Drawing flap pattern

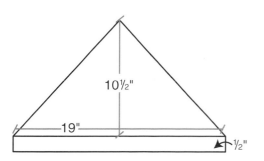

Add ½" to base.

2 Use the pattern to cut a triangle from each flap fabric and the interfacing. Fuse the interfacing to the wrong side of one flap.

3 Sew the base of each flap to the upper edge of a pillow panel.

4 Beginning at the center of the lower edge, apply the cord lip to the front pillow/flap panel.

5 Sew the front and back panels together, aligning edges and the flap/panel stitching line and leaving an opening in the lower edge for turning.

6 Trim the corners, turn right side out and press. Sew the base of the flaps together, stitching in the seamline.

7 Insert the pillow form and slipstitch the opening closed.

8 Cut the tassel loop ends and knot securely at the top of the tassel. Apply seam sealant to the ends and let it dry. Hand sew the knot to the cord at the flap tip.

Four-flap Envelope

Finished size: 18" square

Materials:

- 18"-square pillow form
- 1¾ yd. of floral print for flaps and back
- ⅝ yd. of check for front
- 2¼ yd. of 2" bullion fringe
- 6" of matching brush fringe
- Medium-weight fusible interfacing
- Pattern tracing cloth
- Yardstick or long quilter's ruler
- Permanent fabric adhesive

To make an envelope flap exactly fit the edge of a square pillow panel, you must either add a seam allowance extension as for the Reversible Envelope Pillow or cut the triangle base wide to compensate for the angle. So, what happens if the flap base is cut the same length as the panel edge? After the flap side seams are sewn, the flap will be shorter than the panel by at least 1". While this would be undesirable for many envelope pillows, it gives this pillow its character by revealing the fabric beneath.

Instructions:

1 Using the yardstick or quilter's ruler, draw a triangular flap pattern with a 19" base and 10½" height from the base center to the tip. Use this pattern to cut eight flaps from the floral print and four flaps from the interfacing. From the floral print, also cut a 19"-square panel for the back. From the check fabric, cut a 19"-square panel for the front.

2 Fuse interfacing to the wrong side of four flaps. For each flap, sew an interfaced panel to a panel without interfacing along the side edges, leaving the base edge open. Trim the seam allowance at the point; turn right side out and press. Baste the open edges together.

3 Center each flap on an edge of the check pillow panel and baste in place. With the fringe toward the inside, baste the fringe header to the floral back panel.

4 Sew the panels together, leaving an opening in the lower edge for turning. Trim the corners; turn right side out and press. Insert the pillow form and slipstitch the opening closed.

5 Glue or hand tack the flap tips to the center of the pillow front.

6 To make the center pom-pom, roll up and glue the brush fringe header into a circle. Let the glue dry, then glue to the center front.

Flange Pillows

A flange pillow is made with an oversized knife-edge cover that's topstitched close to the pillow form to make a self-fabric border. You can make the flange as narrow or as deep as you like, and in any pillow shape.

The easiest way to make a flange pillow is to simply sew two panels of the same fabric together, then topstitch around the pillow form area. A back overlap closure makes it easy to insert the form and eliminates the need to topstitch after the pillow form is in place.

For added interest, you can dress up your flange pillows as shown by adding a contrasting or decorative border to any size center panel.

Solid Panel with Striped Flange

Finished size: 24" square

Materials:

- 18"-square pillow form
- ¾ yd. striped fabric
- ¾ yd. coordinating solid

Instructions:

1. From the stripe, cut four identical 9" x 25" strips with the stripe running lengthwise. From the solid, cut one 10" square for the front; cut one 25" x 14½" panel and one 25" x 16" panel for the back overlap.

2. Refer to General Techniques page 26 to overlap the back panels to make a 25" square. Topstitch 3" of the overlap closed, 3" at the upper and lower edges.

3. For the front panels, center a border strip on each edge and sew in place, mitering the corners.

4. Sew the front and back panels together. Trim the corners; turn right side out and press. Topstitch 3" from the outer edges.

5. Insert the pillow form through the back overlap.

Print Panel with Blue Flange

Finished size: 20" square

Materials:

- 16"-square pillow form
- ⅛ yd. of print
- ½ yd. of coordinating solid

Instructions:

1. From the print, cut one 17" square for the front panel; cut one 17" x 10½" panel and one 17" x 12" panel for the back overlap. From the blue fabric, cut eight 3" x 21" strips.

2. Refer to General Techniques page 26 to overlap the back panels to make a 17" square; baste the overlap together at the upper and lower edges.

3. For the front and back panels each, center a border strip on each edge and sew in place, mitering the corners.

4. Sew the front and back panels together. Trim the corners; turn right side out and press. Topstitch along the edge of the blue border.

5. Insert the pillow form through the back overlap.

Reversible Double Flange

Finished size: 26" square

Materials:

- 20"-square pillow form
- 1 yd. each of two contrasting prints
- 5½ yd. of brush fringe
- 5 yd. of ¼"-wide decorative ribbon
- Medium weight fusible interfacing
- 1½"-diameter grommets
- Grommet setting tool
- Water-soluble fabric marker

The flange on this reversible pillow is created by lacing decorative ribbon through grommets instead of sewing. The front and back of this pillow are assembled separately, each with two contrasting fabrics and a fringed edge. Simply unlace, flip each panel over to reveal the contrasting side and lace up.

Instructions:

1 From each print and the interfacing, cut two 25" squares. Fuse the interfacing to two squares of the same print.

2 To assemble each panel, use basting tape to apply fringe along the edges of the square without inter-facing. Sew to the interfaced square, leaving an opening for turning. Trim the corners, turn right side out and press. Slipstitch the opening closed.

3 Complete one panel at a time to mark and apply the grommets. To mark the grommet placements, measure in 3" from the fabric edge and mark 16 evenly spaced placements. Follow the grommet manufacturer's instructions to center and apply a grommet over each mark.

4 Place the panel with the grommets on top of the remaining panel with the edges aligned. Mark through the grommet openings onto the underlying panel. Apply a grommet to the second panel at each mark.

Spaced grommets

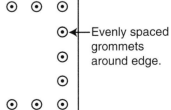

—Evenly spaced grommets around edge.

5 With the pillow form in the center, use ribbon to lace the panels together. Tie the ribbon ends into a bow.

Flanged Pillow Shams

Finished size: 26" x 32"

Materials for each sham:

- 1½ yd. of decorator fabric
- 3½ yd. of 2" bullion fringe
- Cotton batting
- Water-soluble fabric marker

These flanged pillow shams for a standard- or queen-size bed pillow are based on the same technique as flange throw pillows, with a deeper overlap in the back. A layer of fleece batting is added to the front panel for extra plushness, and to add stability to the flange.

Instructions:

1 From the fabric and batting each, cut one 27" x 33" rectangle for the sham front. From the fabric only, cut one 27" x 18" panel and one 27" x 22" panel for the back overlap.

2 Baste the fleece batting to the wrong side of the front panel.

3 Refer to General Techniques page 26 to overlap the back panels to make a 27" x 32" rectangle. Topstitch 3" of the overlap closed at the upper and lower edges.

4 Sew the front and back panels together. Trim the corners, turn right side out through the overlap and press.

Embellished Fabric Designs

Whether you're embellishing the motifs of a fabric design or using trims or appliqués to create your own designs, letting your imagination be carried away is half of the fun. Try some of the following techniques to get started, and you'll be surprised by the new ideas you'll think of.

Tropical Tapestry Pillow

Finished size: 24" x 27"

Materials:

- Tapestry panel
- Home décor fabric cut to tapestry panel size for back panel
- Muslin cut to tapestry panel size
- Fusible batting cut to tapestry panel size
- Decorative eyelash thread
- Heat-applied crystals and applicator tool
- Polyester fiberfill
- Hand-sewing needle

Tapestry panels like this are ready and waiting to inspire your creativity. Readily found in the fabric store home décor areas, these panels often feature motifs and details that are ideal for embellishing, as well as borders suitable for making a self-fabric continuous flange. This panel, for example, features three decorative borders, any of which could have been made into the outside flange.

Instructions:

1 Place the tapestry panel right side down on a flat surface. Layer the batting and muslin on top with the edges aligned. Follow the batting manufacturer's instructions to fuse the layers together.

2 Determine the motifs you want to outline stitch— for this panel, I stitched along the leopard and border outlines and accented random branches with stitching.

3 Refer to "Quilted Dimensions" on page 35 to outline stitch the motifs.

4 Trim the edges of the layers evenly and square the corners.

5 Thread the hand-sewing needle with the eyelash thread. Stitch along the border using a running stitch.

6 Follow the manufacturer's instructions to apply crystals to the leopard eyes, border corners and random flowers and leaves.

7 Sew the tapestry panel to the back panel, leaving an opening for turning. Turn right side out and press the edges.

8 To create the flange, pin then sew the layers together along the inside edges of the outer border, leaving an opening that corresponds with the outer edge opening.

9 Stuff the pillow with fiberfill. Push the fiberfill away from the open flange seam and continue sewing it closed. Slipstitch the outer opening closed.

Palm Tree Diamonds

Finished size: 12" x 16"

Materials:
- 12" x 16" pillow form
- ½ yd. of home décor fabric with diagonal lines
- 1¾ yd. of loop fringe with lip
- Seven wood buttons
- Tapestry needle

The diagonal lines on this palm-tree print fabric create intersections that are perfect for accenting with yarn tufts and buttons. Look for buttons that seem to suit the mood of the fabric—these wood buttons have a tropical ambience that relates them to the fabric. To make yarn tufts that perfectly match the trim, purchase a small amount of extra trim to cut apart.

Instructions:

1 From the home décor fabric, cut two 13" x 17" panels.

2 Cut two 17" trim lengths. Sew a trim length to each short edge of the front pillow panel.

3 Place the front panel on a flat surface. Refer to the photo and evenly arrange the buttons on alternating line intersections; sew in place.

4 To make the yarn tufts, cut the remaining loop fringe from the lip. Cut into eight 3" lengths. For each length, use the tapestry needle to stitch in and out of the fabric at a line intersection, pulling the yarn ends even. Tie into a knot and trim the ends as needed.

5 Sew the panels together, leaving an opening in one short end to turn. Turn and slipstitch the opening closed.

Ribbon-trimmed Bee Print

Finished size: 12" x 16"

Materials:

- 12" x 16" pillow form
- ½ yd. of decorator fabric with repeating motif
- 1¾ to 2 yd. of decorative gimp
- 1¾ yd. of 2" bullion fringe
- Self-adhesive, double-sided basting tape

Any fabric with single motifs that repeat evenly is a perfect candidate for embellishing with diagonal rows of ribbon or trim between the motifs. Let the size of the design and the pillow be your guide when deciding much gimp to purchase and how close to space the trim rows.

Instructions:

1 From the fabric, cut two 13" x 16" panels with the motif repeat centered.

2 Place the front panel on a flat surface. Using the fabric motifs as a guide, plan the placement of the gimp strips before cutting. Cut and use basting tape to adhere the strips, then topstitch in place close to each trim edge.

3 With the fringe toward the center, baste the header to the front panel edges.

4 Sew the panels together, leaving an opening for turning. Trim the corners, turn right side out, and press.

5 Insert the pillow form and slipstitch the opening closed.

Couched Fall Leaves

Finished size: 12" square

Materials:

- 16" pillow form
- ½ yd. silk dupioni fabric for pillow
- ¼ yd. contrasting fabric for ruched welting
- Seven 4" x 5" scraps of real or faux suede in assorted colors for leaves
- 2 yd. of ½"-diameter cotton filler cording
- 2 yd. of narrow twisted metallic cording
- Self-adhesive, double-sided basting tape
- Chalk pencil
- Machine cording foot

Appliqué doesn't get any easier than this! Thanks to the non-fraying nature of Ultrasuede, no edge finish is required for the leaves, and the couched cording stems secure them to the pillow. A cording foot simplifies the technique even more and enables you to apply the free-form stem design in an easy, flowing design.

1 From the pillow fabric, cut two 17" panels with tapered corners. From the welting fabric, cut three 3" x 36" strips. Trace the leaf patterns on page 124 and cut out seven leaves from Ultrasuede.

2 Referring to the photo, arrange the leaves on the pillow front; adhere with basting tape. Use the chalk pencil to draw veins on the leaves and a flowing stem connecting the leaves. Cut a length of cording the same length as each separate vein and stem.

3 Refer to "Couching" on page 38 to couch the metallic cording to the stem and vein lines. Begin and end stems under the leaves wherever possible.

4 Sew the short ends of the welting fabric together to make one long strip. Wrap the strip loosely around the cotton filler cording with wrong sides together and raw edges aligned. Baste to the end of the welting strip, stitching ½" from the raw edges and continuously sliding the fabric up on the cording as you stitch.

5 Arrange the gathers evenly and baste the welting to the edges of the front panel.

6 Sew the front and back panels together, leaving an opening for turning. Turn right side out, insert the pillow form and slipstitch the opening closed.

Chenille Ruffled Pillow

Finished size: 28" diameter

Materials:

- 16" round pillow form
- 1 yd. of chenille
- 2" x 4" scrap of cotton print Chenille By The Inch™ trim: light pink (Cotton Candy), dark pink (Raspberry), green (Key Lime Pie), Yellow (Lemon Ice), light blue (Gumdrop), dark blue (Blueberry), light purple (Jelly Bean), dark purple (Eggplant)
- Chenille brush and cutting guide
- Tear-away stabilizer (if needed)
- 1½ yd. of pom-pom fringe
- Two 1¼" covered button forms
- Waxed button thread
- Upholstery needle
- Spray bottle of water
- Water-soluble fabric marker

This soft, fluffy pillow combines chenille fabric with Chenille By The Inch trim for a look that's reminiscent of yesteryear's chenille bedspreads. An oversized ruffle adds to its comfort appeal.

Instructions:

1 From the chenille fabric, cut two 17"-diameter circles. Cut 13"-wide strips across the width of the fabric to equal a length of 100" for the ruffle.

2 Brush a scrap of the chenille fabric to test. If the chenille pulls out of the backing fabric, use tear-away stabilizer under the chenille trim.

3 Referring to the photo and the pattern on page 121, draw three evenly spaced flowers on one chenille fabric circle. Position the top of each flower 3" from the center of the panel. Draw a leaf on each side of each flower.

4 Follow the "Faux Chenille Strips" instructions on page 39 to cut, apply, and brush the chenille trim.

5 Sew the short ends of the chenille ruffle strips together to make a continuous circle. Fold the strip in half lengthwise with wrong sides together and raw edges aligned; baste the edges together. Refer to the "General Techniques" on page 23 to gather the edge over cording.

6 Place the ruffle on the front pillow panel with the ruffle toward the center. Pull the gathers to evenly fit the edge; baste in place.

7 Sew the front and back panels together, leaving an opening for turning. Insert the pillow form and slipstitch the opening closed.

8 Follow the manufacturer's instructions to cover the buttons with fabric. Tuft the pillow center with a button on each side.

9 Glue pom-pom fringe around the front button and pillow edges.

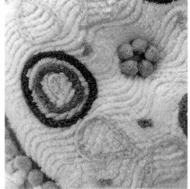

Artistic Elements

Let hand-painted, dyed, or woven fabrics and handmade buttons speak for themselves when you create pillows using these artful materials.

The best design is one with minimal details that doesn't distract from the artistic elements.

Handwoven Panels with Painted Tassel

Finished size: 14" square

Materials:

- 14" pillow form
- ½ yd. of handwoven fabric
- Decorative tassel

This pillow owes its wonderful fringed edges to the natural characteristics of the hand-dyed and woven fabric. The loose weave and dyed yarns give the simple piecing an artistic effect. A tassel with a hand-painted top provides the perfect finishing touch.

Instructions:

1 From the fabric, cut one 16" square for the back and four 9" squares for the front.

2 With wrong sides together and using a 1" seam allowance, sew the front squares together to make a 16" square panel.

3 Sew the front to the back with wrong sides together, using a 1" seam allowance; leave an opening to insert the pillow form.

4 Insert the pillow form and continue the stitching line to sew the opening closed.

5 Snip the 1" seam allowances to the stitching line at 1" intervals.

6 Remove the lengthwise yarns to the stitching line to create fringe.

7 Sew a tassel to the center front.

Stamped Handwoven Envelope

Finished size: 12" x 16"

Materials:

- 12" x 16" pillow for
- ½ yd. of handwoven fabric
- 2¼" x 5" piece of real or faux suede
- 3 raku buttons

This fabric, hand-dyed and woven by the same textile artist, features stamped designs for additional interest. It's paired with handmade raku buttons to create a pillow that's basic in construction, but extraordinary in creative appeal.

Instructions:

1 From the handwoven fabric, cut one 26" x 18" rectangle for the pillow. From the suede, cut three ⅞" x 5" strips for the button loops.

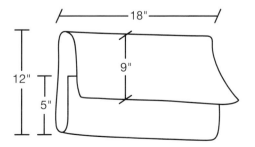

2 Topstitch along the 18" edges, stitching 1" from the edge. With wrong sides together, fold the lower topstitched edge up 5" and the upper edge down 9", overlapping the lower panel.

3 Pin, then sew the side edges, using a 1" seam allowance. Clip the side and flap edges to the seamline at 1" intervals. Fray the fabric to the stitching line to make fringe.

4 Fold each suede strip in half lengthwise and topstitch close to the edge. Sew the ends together to make a loop.

5 Refer to the photo to evenly space and tack the button loops to the flap edge. Sew corresponding buttons to the underlying panel.

Handpainted Raw Silk

Finished size: 18" square

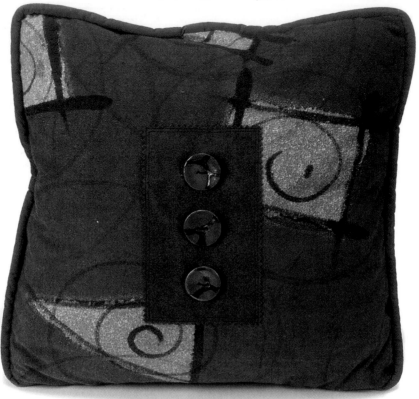

Materials:

- 18" square pillow form
- ⅜ yd. of hand-dyed and painted raw silk
- Ultrasuede: 5½" x 9" rectangle for center
- ⅛ yd. Ultrasuede for welting
- Three raku buttons
- 2 yd. of ½" cotton filler cording
- Self-adhesive, double-sided basting tape
- Rotary cutter with pinking blade

The beautiful hand-dyed and painted raw silk fabric and hand-cast raku buttons are works of art by themselves. They pair together wonderfully, accented subtly by equally luxurious Ultrasuede welting and center appliqué.

Instructions:

1 From the silk, cut two 19"-square panels with tapered corners. From the Ultrasuede for the welting, cut 2" wide strips to equal 38". Trim the edge of the Ultrasuede center rectangle with the rotary cutter and pinking blade.

2 Use basting tape to adhere the pinked Ultrasuede rectangle to the center of the front pillow panel. Topstitch the edges in place. Evenly space and sew the buttons to the rectangle.

3 Wrap the welting strip around the cording with wrong sides together, overlapping the strip ends as needed to complete the length. Baste the edges together.

4 Sew the front and back panels together, leaving an opening for turning. Turn right side out, insert the pillow form and slipstitch the opening closed.

You don't have to begin with fabric yardage to make pillows. Keep an eye out for place mats, doilies, and other linens that have pillow potential. Look for details such as scalloped edges, printed borders, and quilting.

Ribbon-trimmed Place Mat Panel

Finished size: 13" x 18"

The printed scalloped border on these place mats makes them ideal for creating a double-flange look. Couched hand-dyed ribbon hides a slight unevenness in the printing and gives the pillow a finished touch.

Materials:

- Two quilted place mats with scalloped edges and printed border
- 3 yd. of ¼"-wide hand-dyed ribbon
- Polyester fiberfill
- Self-adhesive, double-sided basting tape
- Machine cording foot

Instructions:

1 Use basting tape to adhere the place mats together along the inner edge of the printed border.

2 Refer to "Couching" on page 38 and use the cording foot to couch the ribbon along the edge of the border, stitching through both place mats. Begin at a corner and pull the ribbon up to form loops between the stitches as you sew. Stop sewing 4" from the beginning corner, stuff the pillow with fiberfill, and continue couching the ribbon to close the pillow.

Folded Place Mat with Buttoned Tassel

Finished size: 10" x 14"

This topper is easy to make by simply folding a place mat in half with the edges uneven. Wrap it over a second folded place mat, add an interesting button and tassel, and there you have it—an instant pillow.

Materials:

- Quilted place mat, printed, scalloped edges
- Quilted place mat, solid-color, straight edges
- 1½" button
- 3" tassel
- Polyester fiberfill
- Permanent fabric adhesive

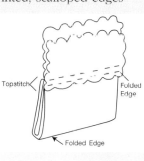

Instructions:

1 For the pillow base, fold the solid-color place mat in half crosswise and topstitch the side edges together. Stuff with fiberfill to 2" from the upper edge.

2 To add the topper, fold the print place mat crosswise with the ends 2" apart. Sew the top end in place. Pin the folded edge to the open edges of the solid-color place mat, overlapping the edge 2½". Topstitch in place close to the folded edge and again ½" from the edge.

3 Fold the double-scallop edge of the topper to the front of the base and glue in place. Sew a tassel to the center front then sew on a button above the tassel.

Floor Pillows

Whether you enjoy sitting on the floor or need extra seating for guests, comfort reigns with an elegant touch when you make these silk dupioni floor pillows.

Tufted Knife Edge

Finished size: 30" square

Materials:

- 1¾ yd. of silk dupioni
- 32 buttons, 1¼" diameter
- Light weight fusible interfacing
- Polyester fiberfill
- Waxed button thread
- Upholstery needle
- Fabric marker

Instructions:

1 Cut two 31"-square panels each from the silk dupioni and interfacing.

2 Fuse the interfacing to the wrong side of the panels. Sew the panels together, leaving an opening for turning and stuffing. Trim the corners, turn right-side out and press.

3 To mark each panel for tufting, use the fabric marker and begin 6" from the edges. Mark four rows of four tufts each, with the marks spaced 6" apart.

4 Beginning at the edge opposite the opening, lightly stuff the pillow 3" past the first row of tuft marks. Refer to the tufting instructions on page 29 and make a tuft with buttons at each mark. Add more stuffing until the section is firmly stuffed. Repeat stuffing and tufting one row at a time to complete the pillow.

5 Slipstitch the opening closed.

Faced Box Edge

Finished size: 25" square

Materials:

- 1½ yd. silk dupioni for panels
- ¾ yd. silk dupioni for boxing strip and facing
- Light-weight fusible interfacing
- Polyester fiberfill

Instructions:

1 From the silk dupioni and interfacing each, cut two 26" squares for the panels, four 5" x 25" strips for the boxing strip and eight 1½" x 26" strips for the facing. Fuse each interfacing piece to the wrong side of the corresponding silk piece.

2 Sew the ends of four facing strips together, mitering the ends, to make a square facing. (See mitered border strips on page 54.) Repeat for the four remaining strips.

3 Sew each set of facing strips to a pillow panel with right sides together and edges aligned. Turn the facing right-side out and press the seam.

4 Sew the short edges of the boxing strip together to make a continuous strip. Aligning the corners, sew the boxing strip edges to inner edges of the facing strips, leaving an opening for turning. Trim the corners; turn right-side out and press. Topstitch ½" from the edges of each panel to create the flange.

5 Over-stuff the pillow with fiberfill. Slipstitch the opening closed.

CHAPTER 5

Cushions

Have a seat—and make it a comfortable one, please. It's sure to be when you add a permanent or loose cushion. From chairs, stools, benches, and window seats to your favorite pet's bed, a cushion adds a practical and attractive finishing touch. Like pillows, all loose cushions are either knife-edge or box-edge variations, and can feature a variety of edge finishes ranging from welting or trim to pleated or gathered ruffles and prairie points.

The first step in making any cushion is to accurately measure the form or surface to be covered and make a pattern if needed (see page 16). A layer of batting or flannel wrapped around or placed on top of upholstery foam and secured with spray adhesive for fabric will smooth the edges and give the cushion a fuller appearance. Refer to the General Techniques to make bias strips, cover cording, and to make and apply edge finishes

Knife Edges
Pleated Ruffle Chair Cushion

Finished size: 14" square

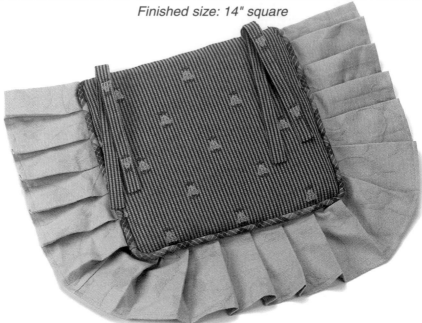

Materials:

- Decorator fabrics: ½ yd. each of three coordinating fabrics for cushion, ruffle and welting
- 1 yd. of ½"-diameter cotton filler cord
- 1" x 14" x 14" Nu-Foam® cushion insert
- Tube-turning tool (optional)
- Spray adhesive for fabric

The knife-pleated ruffle on this cushion makes it suitable for a variety of decors. Dress it up or down, depending on the fabric you choose.

Instructions:

1 From the cushion fabric, cut two 15" squares for the panels and four 2½" x 12½" strips for the ties. From the ruffle fabric, cut two 6½"-wide strips to equal 84" long when pieced together. From the welting fabric, cut an 18" square for the bias strips.

2 Make continuous bias strips and cover the filler cord to make welting. Baste to the front and side edges of the top panel.

3 Sew the ruffle strips together to make an 84"-long strip. Finish the side and lower edges and pleat the strip with 1"-deep knife pleats spaced 2" apart. Baste to the front and side edges of the top panel over the welting.

4 To make the ties, fold each fabric strip in half lengthwise with right sides together. Sew the long edges and one short edge together using a ¼" seam allowance. Trim the corners, turn right-side out and press. Stack two ties with edges aligned and pin the raw edges together; repeat for the two remaining ties.

  Aligning the ties' raw edges and the bottom panel back edge, baste each set of ties to the panel right side, 1½" from the side edge.

5 Baste the welting, then the ruffle strip to the front and side edges of the top cushion panel's right side.

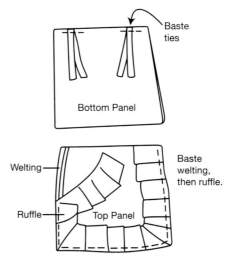

6 Sew the cushion panels together, leaving an opening in the center of the back edge. Trim the corners and turn right-side out. Top the cushion insert with a layer of batting adhered with spray adhesive; insert in the cover and slipstitch the opening closed.

Chair Cushion with Prairie Points

Finished size: 18" deep x 20" wide

Materials:

- 18" x 20" chair cushion pillow form
- ¾ yd. decorator fabric for cushion
- ½ yd. decorator fabric for welting
- ¼ yd. each of two fabrics for prairie points
- 1 yd. of ¼"-diameter cotton filler cord
- 2 yd of ¼"-diameter twisted cording
- 8" of ½"-wide grosgrain ribbon
- 12 small feathers
- Permanent fabric adhesive
- Fabric marker

This plush cushion with its prairie points and feather-trimmed ties lends a casual, country look to any chair. It could also be tufted to accentuate the depth of the cushion.

Instructions:

1 From the cushion fabric, cut two 19" x 21" panels. From the welting fabric, cut one 18" square for the bias strips. From each prairie point fabric, cut and piece two 4½"-wide strips to a 60" length.

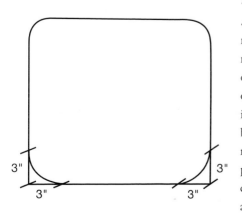

2 To round the cushion corners identically, make a mark 3" on each side of one corner. Cut in a curve between the marks. Fold the panel to use the curved corner as a guide to cut the remaining corners.

3 Make continuous bias strips and cover the filler cord. Baste to the edges of the top panel.

4 Make the prairie points and baste to the edges of the top panel.

5 To make the ties, cut the twisted cording length in half. Glue three feathers to the end of each length. Cut the grosgrain ribbon into eight 2" lengths; glue a length around each cord end, covering the feather ends. Knot each cord end at the top of the ribbon wrap.

6 Fold each cord length with the ends offset by 2" to 3". Baste the fold to the back edge of the bottom cushion panel at the inside edge of the curve.

7 Sew the panels together, leaving an opening in the center back. Turn right-side out and insert the cushion. Slipstitch the opening closed.

Tufted Stool Cushion
with Chair Ties

Finished size: 13" diameter

Materials:

- ½ yd. of toile decorator fabric
- 1½ yd. each of ⅜"-diameter twisted cord with lip
- 1½ yd. 1" brush fringe with lip
- ½ yd. of yarn
- 4 chair ties with tassels
- Polyester fiberfill
- Upholstery needle
- Fabric marker

The style of this lightly-stuffed, tufted cushion with chair ties could be used for almost any stool, bench, or chair where a more delicate effect is desired.

Instructions:

1 From the fabric, cut two 14" circular panels, centering the toile motifs.

2 Place the bottom panel right-side up on the seat. Mark the placement of each chair tie at a leg. Fold each chair tie in half and pin the fold to a mark.

3 Baste the cord with lip, then the fringe, to the edges of the top panel.

4 Sew the top and bottom panels together, leaving an opening for turning. Clip the curves and turn right-side out. Stuff lightly with fiberfill and slipstitch the opening closed.

5 To add the tufts, mark four points spaced 5" apart to form a square in the center of the top panel. Use the needle and yarn to make a tied-yarn tuft at each point.

6 Place the cushion on the stool, wrap the ties around the legs and tie at the front of each leg.

Fitted Stool Cushion with Ruffle

Finished size: 15" diameter

Sewing Fitted Band to Panel

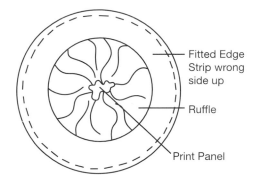

Fitted Edge Strip wrong side up

Ruffle

Print Panel

Materials:

• ½ yd. of decorator print for top panel and fitted edge
• ⅝ yd. of decorator check for ruffle
• ½ yd. of muslin for bottom panel
• 1½ yd. of 2" brush fringe with header
• Batting
• 1 yd. of ¼"-wide elastic

If you need a stool cushion that won't shift when it's sat upon, choose this fitted style. An elasticized fabric band holds it securely to the stool top, and it's equally attractive with or without a ruffle. For fun, paint your stool to echo the colors of the fabric.

Instructions:

1 Cut one 16"-diameter circle each from the decorator print, fusible batting, and muslin. From the decorator print, also cut one 3" x 48" strip for the fitted edge. From the decorator check, cut two 9" x 41" strips for the ruffle.

2 With the batting in the middle and edges aligned, fuse the fabric circles with wrong sides together. Baste the fringe header to the print panel edges, stitching through all layers.

3 Sew the short edges of the ruffle strips together to make a continuous ruffle; hem one long edge. Gather the ruffle to fit the circumference of the fused panels. Arrange the gathers evenly and baste to the edge of the print panel/fringe, with the ruffle toward the center.

4 Sew the short edges of fitted edge strip together to make a continuous band. With the edges even, sew right-side down to the edge of the print panel/fringe/ruffle.

5 To make the elastic casing, serge or finish one long edge of the fitted band strip with zigzag stitches. Press under ½" and topstitch close to the outer edge, leaving an opening to insert the elastic. Thread the elastic through the casing. Place the cover on the stool and adjust the elastic to the desired tightness. Remove from the stool and sew the elastic ends together. Topstitch the casing opening closed.

6 To reduce the seam allowance bulk, serge ¼" from the seamline or trim and grade the seam allowances. Turn the fitted band to the bottom of the cushion and place over the stool seat.

Box Edges
Dog Bed Cushion

Finished size: 20" x 30" x 5"

Photo by Kevin May.

Materials:
- 1 yd. of decorator toile for top and bottom panels
- 1¼ yd. of decorator check for box edge and welting
- 1½ yd. of muslin or cotton sheeting for insert
- 5¾ yd of ½"-diameter cotton filler cord
- ½ yd. of sew-on Velcro®
- Clear paw-print stamp
- Textile paint and stamp pad
- Polyester fiberfill
- Heavy-duty fusible adhesive sheet
- Seam sealant

Every pampered pup needs it's own toile dog bed for napping in style, and my little bulldog Lucy loves this one. The removable cover of this bed features a Velcro® closure embellished with a dog bone appliqué. Stamped paw prints add a finishing touch to the boxing strip.

Instructions:

1 From the toile, cut two 21" x 31" rectangular panels and two 3" x 12" strips for the appliqué. From the check, cut two 6" x 31" strips for the box strip sides, one 6" x 21" strip for one box edge end, two 5" x 21" strips for the box edge overlap end and one 24" square for the bias strips. From the muslin, cut two 21" x 31" panels, two 6" x 31" strips and two 6" x 21" strips for the insert.

2 Use the check fabric square to make continuous bias strips; cover the filler cord to make welting. Baste to the edges of both toile panels.

3 Refer to the General Techniques on page 26 and use the 6" x 21" strips to make an overlapping Velcro closure for one box strip end panel.

4 Trace the dog bone pattern on page 123 onto the fusible-adhesive paper side. Fuse to the wrong side of a toile strip and cut out. Remove the paper backing and fuse to the wrong side of the remaining toile strip.

Cut out and topstitch close to the edges. Apply seam sealant to the appliqué edges and let it dry. Refer to the photo and sew the appliqué to the closure edge.

5 Sew the short ends of the boxing strips together to make a 20" x 30" rectangle. Stamp the strips with the paw print stamp and textile ink as instructed on page 39.

6 Sew the panels to the box strips, aligning edges and corners. Trim the corners and turn right side-out through the overlapping closure.

7 To make the insert, sew the muslin box strips together to make a continuous strip. Sew the panels to the box strip edges, matching corners and leaving an opening for turning. Turn and stuff with fiberfill; slipstitch the opening closed. Place the insert in the dog bed cover.

Bench and Window Seat Cushions

Finished size: Custom Fit

Materials:

- Yardage needed to make two panels and box strip in depth of your choice, plus ⅛" for each seam allowance
- Yardage needed for desired ruffle length and width
- Yardage needed for fabric for bias strips
- Cotton filler cord to fit perimeter of one or both panels
- Upholstery foam in desired thickness
- Batting
- Spray adhesive for fabric
- Tracing paper
- Permanent medium-tip marker

Box-edge cushions for benches and window seats are all constructed in the same manner, some with the addition of welting or a ruffle. Because these cushions will usually be a custom size, the most important step is to accurately measure the surface the cushion will fit.

Instructions:

1. Trace the bench or window seat surface onto tracing paper and cut out. Using the pattern as a guide, use the marker to draw the outline on the upholstery foam. Cut the foam along the lines with an electric knife. Spray the foam with adhesive spray and wrap with a layer of batting to soften the edges.

2. Use the pattern to cut out the top and bottom fabric panels, adding ½" to each edge for a seam allowance.

3. Cut a boxing strip equal to the cushion depth, plus 1" for the width. For the length, measure the cushion perimeter, plus 1"; piece the strips if needed to achieve the necessary length.

4. Follow the General Techniques to make welting or a ruffle, if desired, and baste to the panel edges.

5. Sew the box strip to the top panel. At each corner, press a fold in the box strip. Sew the box strip to the bottom panel, aligning the fold with corners and leaving an opening for inserting the wrapped cushion. Trim the corners and turn right-side out. Insert the cushion and slipstitch the opening closed.

Ruffled Stool Cushion

Finished size: 14" diameter

Materials:
- ½ yd. each of print for panels and check for welting
- ⅓ yd. of windowpane check for welting and ruffle
- ¼ yd. of solid for box strip
- 1¼ yd. of cotton filler cord
- 1"-thick upholstery foam
- 2 yd. of ribbon for ties
- Batting
- Electric knife
- Medium-tip permanent marker
- Electric knife

This tie-on cushion adds height to the stool and can be made with or without the gathered ruffle.

Instructions:

1 Use the marker to draw a 14" circle on the upholstery foam. Use the electric knife to cut out the circle for a cushion.

2 From the print, cut two 15"-circles for the panels. From the check, cut one 18" square for the bias strips. From the windowpane check, cut two 5½" x 45" strips for the ruffle. From the solid fabric, cut one 2" x 45" strip for the box strip. From the batting, cut one 15" circle.

3 Baste the batting to the wrong side of the top panel.

4 Make continuous bias strips and cover the filler cord with the check fabric to make welting. Baste to the edges of the top panel.

5 Place the bottom panel on the stool and mark each tie placement at a stool leg. Cut the ribbon into four equal lengths; fold each length in half and tack the fold to a placement mark.

6 Sew the ruffle strips together to make a continuous circle. Hem one edge then gather the remaining edge to 44". Baste to the edge of the bottom panel.

7 Sew the short edges of the box strip together. Sew one edge to the top panel. Sew the remaining edge to the bottom panel, leaving an opening for the cushion. Turn right-side out, insert the form, and slipstitch the opening closed.

Ruched Edge Chair Cushion

Finished size: Custom fit

This chair cushion has a contemporary flair with its ruched box edge and tabs that wrap around the outer slats of the chair back. Like the bench cushion, this style needs to be custom fitted to your chair for proper placement of the tabs.

Instructions:

1 Trace the chair seat onto tracing paper, marking a tab placement at each outer chair back slat; cut out the pattern. Trace the shape onto the foam and use an electric knife to cut. Spray the foam with adhesive and wrap with a layer of batting.

2 Using the pattern, cut the top and bottom panels from the windowpane check, adding a ½" seam allowance to each edge; mark each tab placement with a pin. From the check, cut a square for the bias strips.

3 From the stripe, cut the boxing strips and tabs. Measure the cushion pattern front and side edges between the tab placement marks; cut a 2"-wide box strip equal to twice this measurement. Measure the back edge of the cushion pattern between the tab placement marks and cut a 2"-wide strip equal to twice this measurement. Cut four 2" x 8" strips for the tabs.

4 Make the welting and baste it to the edges of both panels.

Materials:

- Windowpane check in yardage to cover top and bottom of cushion, plus 1"
- Stripe in yardage to cut a 2"-wide strip twice the length of the cushion perimeter plus 32" for the ruched box strip and tabs
- ⅜"-diameter cotton filler cord in length equal to twice the cushion perimeter
- Check print in enough yardage to create welting
- 1"-thick upholstery foam
- Batting
- Spray adhesive for fabric
- 8" length of sew-on Velcro®
- Tracing paper
- Electric knife

5 To make each set of tabs, sew two fabric strips together, leaving an opening for turning. Trim the corners, turn right-side out, and press. Slipstitch the opening closed. Sew Velcro halves to the opposite sides of the tab ends.

6 Gather the front/side boxing strip along both long edges to fit the cushion sides and front between the marks. Baste the edges to secure the gathers. Repeat for the back strip, making it fit the back edge between the marks.

Sewing Velcro to ties

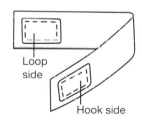

Loop side

Hook side

7 Fold each tab strip in half. Pin the folds to the ends of the back boxing strip. Sew the back boxing strip to the side strips, securing the tab fold in the seam.

Sew side strips and tabs

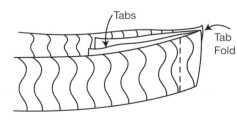

Tabs

Tab Fold

8 Sew the boxing strip to the top panel, aligning the tabs with the placement marks.

Repeat for the bottom panel, leaving an opening for the cushion. Turn right-side out and insert the cushion. Slipstitch the opening closed.

Outdoor Furniture Cushions

*Finished sizes: box-edge seat cushion, 22" square; box-edge back cushion, 19" x 22";
contemporary box-edge chair cushion, 20" x 22"; bistro chair, custom fit.*

When planning outdoor furniture cushions, it's important to choose fabrics and cushions that are intended for outdoor use. The featured outdoor fabrics are treated to be water-resistant and resist fading from the sunlight. The cushions are made with Nu-Foam—an upholstery foam alternative that won't absorb water and resists mildew.

For the bistro chair, follow the instructions for the box-edge bench cushion to make the set-in cushion.

Box Edge Settee Cushions

Materials for each cushion:

- 4" x 22" Nu-Foam cushion
- ¾ yd. coordinating outdoor decorator fabric for top and bottom panels
- ⅜ yd. fabric for boxing strip
- ⅝ yd. fabric for welting
- 5 yd of ¼"-diameter cotton filler cord
- 28"-long upholstery zipper

Instructions:

1 For the 22"-square seat cushion: Cut two 23" squares for the panels. Cut and piece a 5" x 61" strip for the front/sides boxing strip and two 3½" x 28" strips for the zipper boxing strip. Cut a 20" square for the bias strips.

For the 19" x 22" back cushion: Cut two 20" x 23" rectangles for the panels. Cut a 5" x 55" strip for the front/sides boxing strip and two 3½" x 28" strips for the zipper boxing strip. Cut a 20" square for the bias strips.

2 Make continuous bias strips and cover the filler cord to make welting. Baste to the edges of the top and bottom panels. Note: If desired, add welting to only the side and top edges of the back cushions.

3 Follow the General Techniques on page 27 to install the zipper and assemble the boxing strip. Place the strip around the cushion and mark the cushion corners on each edge of the strip; remove from the cushion.

4 Sew the boxing strip to the panels, matching the corners. Turn right-side out through the zippered opening. For the seat cushion, insert the Nu-Foam cushion and zip closed. For the back cushion, trim 3" off one edge of the Nu-Foam cushion and insert it in the cover.

Contemporary
Box Edge Chair Cushion

Materials:

- 4" x 22" Nu-Foam cushion
- ¾ yd. coordinating outdoor decorator fabric for top and bottom panels
- ⅜ yd. fabric for welting
- 2½ yd of ¼"-diameter cotton filler cord
- Pattern tracing cloth
- Permanent marker

This cushion is cut to the shape of the chair seat. Make a pattern to exactly fit your chair.

Instructions:

1 Trace the chair seat onto pattern tracing cloth and cut out. Trace the pattern onto the Nu-Foam cushion and cut out. Trim the cushion edges to round them.

2 To make the panel pattern, use the marker to draw a line around the center of the cushion edge. Place tracing paper over the cushion top and wrap over the edges; pin in place to fit the cushion, making two small pleats at each front corner. Mark the cushion edge center line on the tracing paper.

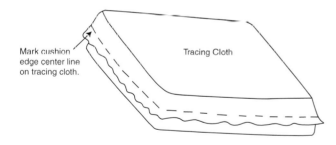

Mark cushion edge center line on tracing cloth.

Tracing Cloth

3 Remove the pattern and add a ½" seam allowance to the traced edge. Use this pattern to cut two panels. Baste the corner pleats in place on each panel.

4 Cut a 13½" square from the welting fabric and cut continuous bias strips. Cover the cord to make welting. Baste the welting to the upper panel edge.

5 Sew the panels together, leaving an opening for the cushion. Insert the cushion and slipstitch the opening closed.

Permanent Cushions

If you love to browse estate sales, there's no need to pass up a bench or chair with a drop-in seat, just because it's seen better days. Look beyond the wear and tear—if it's structurally sound and has interesting design lines, you can easily transform it into an object of beauty with some fabric and paint (see page 40).

Photo by Kevin May. Courtesy of *Creative Machine Embroidery*.

Before

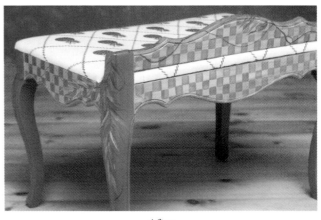

After

Permanent Seat Cushion

Materials:
- Decorator fabric to cover chair, plus 4" for each edge
- Batting
- Staple gun and staples
- Screwdriver
- Upholstery foam (if needed)

Instructions:

1 Turn the chair upside down and remove the screws that hold the wood seat board in place. Use the screwdriver to remove the staples securing the fabric. Carefully remove the fabric cover.

2 Using the fabric cover as a pattern, cut one cover each from the decorator fabric and batting.

3 If the original foam used on the seat board is worn or misshapen, replace it with a new layer of foam cut to the same size.

4 Center the batting, then the fabric, right-side up, on top of the seat. Smooth the fabric over the surface, making certain stripes or directional designs are straight.

5 Carefully turn the board upside down and wrap the fabric edges to the underside. Staple the center of each fabric edge to the board.

6 Make sure the fabric is still straight on the top of the seat, then turn the board back over. Finishing the front edge first, work out from the center staple, to smoothly pull and closely staple the fabric edge in place to 2" from each corner. Repeat for the sides, then the back edge.

7 To secure the corners, wrap the fabric over the corner and ease in place, stapling close together.

8 Trim the fabric ½" beyond the staples. Place in the chair and screw in place.

CHAPTER 6

Tuffets

Like Little Miss Muffet, you, too, can sit on a tuffet. Or, if you prefer, rest your feet on one, or even use it as a little table. Defined by Webster's dictionary as "a low seat," I'm using the word tuffet loosely to include a variety of fun-loving décor accents. They vary from ottoman- to footstool-size, and include styles that range from traditional to whimsical. Some are based on wood boards and chair legs or post finials, others are based on crates, footstools, and even juice cans. The best part? They really are fun to make.

The first step in getting started is to purchase a footstool or crate or head to the home improvement store for wood circles, fence post finials, or chair legs. If you can't find wood circles, ask a lumberyard to cut one for you. Have a staple gun handy, and you're ready to go. All you need to add are fabrics, trims, and padding.

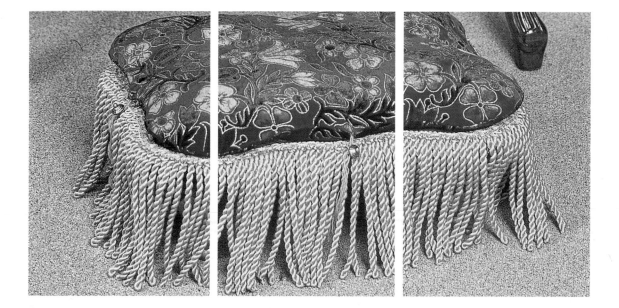

Floral Tuffet with Pleated Skirt

Finished size: 19" high x 21" diameter

Instructions:

1. Mark the four leg placements 1½" from the edge of the wood circle, spacing evenly. Drill a hole slightly smaller than the furniture leg screw at each mark. Apply wood glue to the end of each leg and screw into the hole.

2. Draw a 21" circle on the upholstery foam; mark the circle center on each side of the foam. Use the electric knife to cut out the circle. Glue the foam to the board with fabric adhesive. Curve the top edge of the foam slightly by using the knife to cut off the corner. Note: The edge will be more curved after the fabric is applied.

3. From the floral print and batting each, cut a 34"-diameter circle. From the stripe, cut two 16" strips across the width of the fabric.

4. Sew the striped panels together to create one long strip. Follow the General Techniques on page 24 to press twelve 5½"-wide pleats into the strip, using the stripes as a guide. Sew the short edges together. Serge or zigzag stitch the bottom edge; press under 1" and topstitch. Baste the top edges of the pleats together.

5. Treating the batting and fabric as one, center them over the foam-topped board. Wrap the fabric tightly over the edges at two opposite points and staple underneath the board. Repeat for two points halfway between the first two. Continue pulling the fabric edge tightly over the foam and stapling to the underside, stapling close together, until the entire edge is stapled in place.

6. Slip the pleated skirt over the top of the tuffet with the hemmed edge ½" from the floor. Closely staple the ruffle edge to the edge of the covered board. Trim excess ruffle fabric above the staples, if necessary.

7. Using fabric adhesive, glue the tasseled trim around the tuffet, covering the edge of the ruffle.

Materials:

- 1 yd. floral print fabric
- 1 yd. striped fabric with 5½"-wide design
- 2 yd. of tasseled fringe with decorative header
- 21" of 4"-thick upholstery foam
- Batting
- 21"-diameter circle of ¾"- to 1"-thick wood
- Four 14" screw-in furniture legs
- Permanent medium-tip marker
- Permanent fabric adhesive
- Wood glue
- Electric knife
- Heavy-duty staple gun
- Drill

Mitered Stripe Tuffet
with Gathered Skirt

Finished size: 17" high x 24" diameter

Instructions:

1 Drill a ½"-diameter hole through the center of the wood board. Mark the four leg placements 1½" from the edge of the wood circle, spacing evenly. Drill a hole slightly smaller than the furniture leg screw at each mark. Apply wood glue to the end of each and screw into the hole.

2 Draw a 24" circle on the upholstery foam; mark the circle center on each side of the foam. Use the electric knife to cut out the circle. Use fabric adhesive to glue the foam to the board. Note: The edge will be curved after the fabric is applied.

3 Following the General Techniques for creating mitered stripes on page 35, draw a 39"-diameter circle on paper and make a pattern for cutting each stripe section. Sew the panels together to create the mitered stripes panel. Cut a 39" circle from batting.

4 From the print, cut two 12½" strips across the width of the fabric. Sew the short edges of strips together to create a continuous strip. Serge or zigzag stitch the bottom edge; press under 1" and topstitch. Follow the General Techniques on page 18 to gather the opposite edge to fit the wood circle edge.

5 Treating the batting and fabric as one, center them over the foam topped board. Wrap the fabric tightly over the edges at two opposite points and staple underneath the board. Repeat for two points halfway between the first two. Continue pulling the fabric edge tightly over the foam and stapling to the underside, stapling close together, until the entire edge is stapled in place.

6 Slip the gathered ruffle over the top of the tuffet with the hemmed edge ½" from the floor. Evenly arrange the gathers and closely staple the ruffle edge to the edge of the covered board. Trim excess ruffle fabric above the staples, if necessary.

7 Using fabric adhesive, glue the bullion fringe around the tuffet, covering the edge of the ruffle. Glue gimp to the bullion fringe header.

8 Cover the button with fabric. Follow the tufting instructions on pages 29-31 to tuft the center of the tuffet, using the covered button on the top and the metal button underneath.

Materials:

- 1¼ yd. of striped fabric
- ¾ yd. of coordinating print
- 2¼ yd. each of 6" bullion fringe and decorative gimp
- 24" of 4"-thick upholstery foam
- Batting
- 24"-diameter circle of ¾"- to 1"-thick wood
- Four 12" screw-in furniture legs
- Permanent medium-tip marker
- Permanent fabric adhesive
- Wood glue
- 2" covered buttons
- 1" flat metal buttons
- Upholstery supplies: waxed button thread; long upholstery needle
- Electric knife
- Heavy-duty staple gun
- Drill

Puffy Tuffet

Finished size: 13" x 31"

This casual, puffy tuffet is a perfect size for resting your feet or sitting. Its painted fence-post finial feet are topped with cotton bullion fringe for a touch of whimsy.

Materials:

- 3 yd. of 54"-wide decorator fabric
- 1¼ yd. of 3" cotton bullion fringe
- ¼ yd. of brush fringe
- 31" of 5"-thick upholstery foam
- High-loft polyester batting
- Polyester fiberfill
- 24"-diameter circle of ¾"-thick wood
- Four 6" wood fence post finials
- 2" covered button form
- Permanent medium-tip marker
- Acrylic paint: two colors to coordinate with fabric
- Water-based gloss varnish
- Flat paintbrush
- 12" needle; waxed button thread
- 1" or larger metal button
- Electric knife
- Drill
- Heavy-duty staple gun
- Permanent fabric adhesive
- Wood glue

Instructions:

1 Drill a ½" hole through the center of the wood circle. Mark evenly spaced leg placements on the underside of the board. Drill a hole slightly smaller than the finial screw at each mark. Apply wood glue to the top of the finial and screw into the hole.

2 Draw a 31" circle on the upholstery foam; mark the circle center on each side of the foam. Use the electric knife to cut out the circle. Also cut a 1" hole through the foam at the center marks. Glue the foam to the wood, aligning the center holes.

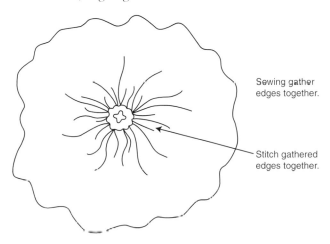

Sewing gather edges together.

Stitch gathered edges together.

3 Cut three 30" strips across the width of the fabric. Sew the short ends of the fabric strips together to form a continuous circle. Tightly gather one long edge and slipstitch the edges together to form a knot.

4 Cut a 60" circle of batting with a 1" hole in the center. Center the batting, then the fabric over the foam with centers aligned. Using the upholstery needle and waxed thread, stitch back and forth through the fabric knot several times, then thread the needle through the hole in the foam and wood. Pull tightly until the fabric knot recedes into the foam; tie the thread ends to a metal button on the bottom of the wood.

5 Lift the fabric and batting, and then pad the foam surface with polyester fiberfill to the desired puffiness. Wrap the fabric and batting around the foam edges, arranging the gathers evenly, and staple to the bottom of the wood base.

6 Cover the button with fabric and glue brush fringe around the edge. Glue into the center of the tuffet.

7 Paint the fence post finials with two coats of acrylic paint and let the paint dry. Dip your finger into the contrasting paint color to add dots to the finials. Let dry, then apply two coats of water base varnish, letting the varnish dry between coats and after the final coat.

8 Cut and glue bullion fringe around the top of each painted foot.

Rounded Floral Tuffet

Finished size: 15-1/2" high x 18" diameter

The roundness of this medium-size tuffet with painted feet adds to its charm. The extra-deep foam surface is rounded with an electric knife before covering, and a pleated edge keeps the cover edge neat and orderly while adding a designer touch.

Materials:

- 1½ yd. of 54"-wide decorator fabric
- 3¼ yd. of pom-pom fringe
- 18" each of 4"- and 5"-thick upholstery foam
- Batting
- 18"-diameter circle of ¾"- to 1"-thick wood
- Four 5½" wood fence-post finials
- Permanent medium-tip marker
- Acrylic paint to coordinate with fabric
- Water-based gloss varnish
- Flat paintbrush
- Electric knife
- Drill
- Heavy duty staple gun
- Permanent fabric adhesive
- Wood glue

Instructions:

1 Mark evenly-spaced placements for the legs on the wood base. Drill a hole slightly smaller than the finial screw at each mark. Apply wood glue to the top of each finial and screw into a hole.

2 Draw an 18" circle on each piece of upholstery foam. Use the electric knife to cut out the circles. Glue one circle on top of the other, using permanent fabric adhesive; glue to the wood base. Let the glue dry. Using the electric knife, trim the top and sides of the foam to a rounded shape.

3 From the fabric and batting each, cut a 45"-diameter circle. Wrap the batting tightly over the foam and staple the edges underneath the wood base. Center the fabric over the foam; pin to the foam around the tuffet, 4" above the base.

4 Evenly pleat the fabric to fit the lower edge, pinning the pleats close to the base. Keeping the pleat folded, wrap the fabric edges under the base and staple in place, stapling closely.

5 Paint the fence post finials with two coats of acrylic paint and let the paint dry. Refer to the photo and paint stripes. Let dry, then apply two coats of water-base varnish, letting the varnish dry between coats and after the final coat.

Pinning fabric to tuffet top

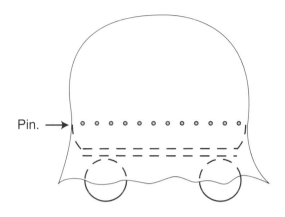

Pin. →

6 Glue two rows of pom-pom fringe around the edge of the covered wood base.

Tufted Rectangular Tuffet

Finished size: 12" x 16" x 20"

Based on a wood plaque, this tufted tuffet is edged with short brush fringe to show its painted gold legs. The result is a dressier look, but the comfort is still there.

Materials:

- ⅔ yd. of floral stripe decorator fabric
- 2 yd. of brush fringe
- 16" x 20" rectangle of 3"-thick upholstery foam
- Batting
- 16" x 20" basswood plaque
- Four 9" furniture legs
- Eight each of ⅝" covered button forms
- 1" metal buttons for tufting
- Gold metallic acrylic paint
- Flat paintbrush
- Upholstery supplies: waxed button thread; long upholstery needle
- Drill
- Heavy duty staple gun
- Permanent fabric adhesive
- Wood glue

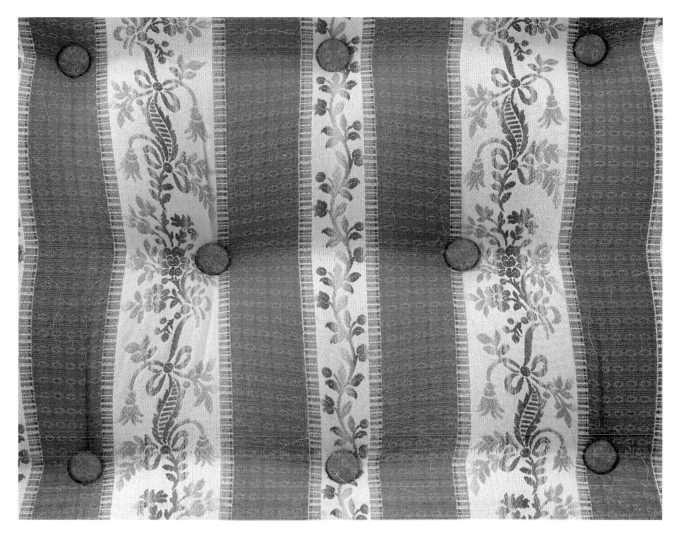

Instructions:

1 On the wood plaque, measure in 1½" from the sides at each corner and mark the leg placement. Drill a hole slightly smaller than the leg screw at each placement mark. Apply wood glue to the top of each leg and screw into a hole. Mark the tufting holes on the plaque and drill a ¼"-diameter hole at each mark.

2 Use fabric adhesive to glue the upholstery foam to the top of the board.

3 From the fabric and batting each, cut a 24" x 28" rectangle. Layer the fabric over the batting; center over the foam. Wrap the batting and fabric tightly over the foam and staple the edges underneath the wood base.

4 Mark tufting placements on the fabric to correspond with the holes in the board. Cover the eight buttons with fabric. Refer to the General Techniques on page 30 and tuft the tuffet top, using the upholstery needle, waxed thread, and buttons.

5 Glue the brush fringe around the lower edge of the sides.

6 Paint the legs with two coats of metallic gold, letting the paint dry between coats.

Marking tufts

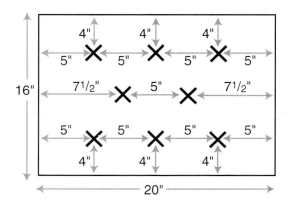

Toile Storage Tuffet

Finished size: 14" x 12" x 16"

Materials:

- 1½ yd. of check for pleats and box cover
- ¾ yd. of stripe for skirt
- ½ yd. of toile for top
- 1¾ yd. of brush fringe
- 12" x 16" rectangle of 2"-thick upholstery foam batting
- 12½" x 16½" basswood plaque
- 11½" x 12" x 16" wood crate
- Permanent fabric adhesive
- Heavy-duty staple gun

Style meets practicality when you upholster a wood storage crate and wood plaque lid. Finished inside and out, it's a perfect place to store books or magazines.

Instructions:

1 From the toile and batting each, cut one 20" x 24" rectangle for the top of the lid. From the stripe, cut four 12½" x 17" rectangles for the skirt. From the check, cut and piece two 15" x 62" strips to cover the inside and outside of the crate, two 13" x17" rectangles for the bottoms of the lid and crate, and four 12½" x 7" rectangles for the corner pleats.

2 To make the lid, glue the foam to the top of the wood plaque. Layer the batting, then the fabric centered over the foam. Wrap the edges tightly to the underside of the board, making a fold at each corner, and staple in place. Press the edges of the 13" x 17" rectangle under ½"; glue the edges to the underside of the lid, covering the raw edges of the toile.

3 To cover the outside of the crate, glue one 15" x 62" strip around the outside of the crate with the fabric edge and crate upper edges aligned; overlap and glue the ends. Wrap the excess fabric to the bottom of the crate and glue in place.

4 To cover the inside of the crate, begin at the center of one edge and glue the fabric strip with 2" of the strip extending above the crate upper edge. At each corner, glue the fabric 1" past the corner, then fold it back on itself to the corner and continue gluing.

5 To cover the upper edge, clip the fabric extension to the crate edge at each corner. Wrap the fabric over the edge and glue. At each corner, spread the fold fullness out to cover the corner and glue in place.

6 Press under the edges of the remaining 13" x 17" rectangle to fit the inside bottom edge of the crate. Glue the edges in place.

7 To make the skirt, alternate and sew the stripe and check skirt panels together to make a continuous circle. Serge or zigzag stitch one long edge, press under ½" and topstitch. At the seams of each check panel, press under a box pleat with the check on the inside; baste the upper edges of the pleat in place.

8 Slide the skirt over the crate, aligning the pleats with the corners. Beginning with the long sides, staple the upper edge of the skirt to the edge of the crate. On each short edge, make a knife pleat with the excess fabric in the center of the edge and staple in place; continue stapling the edge in place.

9 Glue brush fringe around the upper edges of the crate, extending the trim slightly above the edge to prevent a gap when the lid is in place.

Lining crate

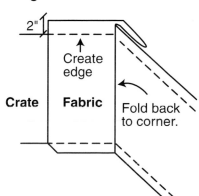

2"

Create edge

Crate Fabric

Fold back to corner.

Velvet Pillow Tuffet

Finished size: 8" x 12" x 16"

Materials:

- ¾ yd. of 45"-wide painted velvet
- 2 yd. 6" gold bullion fringe
- 2 yd. gold metallic looped gimp
- Gold pearle cotton thread
- Four ½" gold buttons or beads
- Polyester fiberfill
- 12" x 16" basswood plaque
- Four 4" gold drapery finials
- Permanent fabric adhesive
- Wood glue
- Heavy-duty staple gun
- Tracing paper
- Velvet pressing cloth

Small and elegant, the pillow on this painted velvet tuffet buttons on its center points to add design interest. The shape of the tuffet and pillow are determined by the Chippendale wood plaque used for the base. Gold curtain finial for feet completes an opulent look.

Instructions:

1 To make a pattern, trace the outline of the board onto tracing paper; add ½" to the edges and cut out. Use the pattern to cut two velvet panels for the pillow. Also cut one panel to cover the board, adding 3" to each edge of the pattern.

2 To make the tuffet base, screw a finial into the bottom of the board, 1½" from the sides of each corner, applying wood glue to the top of the finial.

3 Center the velvet panel over the base and wrap the edges to the wrong side. Staple the fabric edges in place, clipping the excess fabric to the edge of the board at inside curves.

4 Use permanent adhesive to glue the fringe header around the top of the board edges. Glue the gimp to the fringe header.

Clipping excess fabric.

Clip to board edge.

Bottom of Tuffet

5 Sew the velvet pillow panels together, leaving an opening for turning. Clip the curves, trim points and turn right side out. Use a velvet pressing cloth to press the edges. Stuff with polyfill and slipstitch the opening closed.

6 For each button tie, cut three 15" lengths of pearle cotton and fold in half. Tack the fold to the underside of each center side point of the pillow.

7 Tack a button or bead to the corresponding point on the tuffet base. Tie the threads around the button to secure.

Chenille Heart Tuffet

Finished size: 8" x 12" x 16"

Materials:

- ¾ yd. of 60"-wide chenille fabric
- Batting
- 1¾ yd. each of pom-pom fringe
- Chenille By The Inch:
light pink, dark pink, light green, yellow, blue, purple (see page 39)
- 9" x 10" x 10" heart-shaped footstool
- 10" square of 2"-thick uphol-stery foam
- Chenille brush and cutting guide
- Rotary cutter and mat
- Spray bottle of water
- Permanent medium-tip marker
- Permanent fabric adhesive
- Electric knife
- Heavy-duty staple gun
- Tracing paper

Perfect for your favorite little girl, this soft chenille tuffet is based on a heart shaped footstool. Chenille By The Inch and pom-pom fringe give it its charm and make it the perfect companion for the Chenille Ruffle Pillow on page 76.

Instructions:

1 To make a pattern, trace the outline of the stool top onto tracing paper; add 3" to the edges and cut out. Use the pattern to cut one panel each from the chenille fabric and batting for the tuffet top. From the chenille fabric, also cut one 9½" x 60" strip for the ruffle.

2 Referring to the photo and the pattern on page 121, use the fabric marker to draw one flower, three leaves, and accent dot in the center of the chenille heart panel. Follow the "Faux Chenille Strips" instructions on page 39 to cut, apply and brush the chenille trim.

3 Layer the chenille heart panel on the batting panel and center over the top of the stool. Wrap the fabric around the stool edge and staple closely underneath the stool top.

4 Sew the ends of the ruffle strip together to make a continuous strip. Serge or zigzag stitch one edge; turn it under ½" and topstitch in place for the hem. Follow the General Techniques on page 23 to gather the upper edge of the ruffle strip by zigzag stitching over cording.

5 Place the ruffle over the stool and pull the gathers to fit the stool edge. Staple in place around the edge.

6 Glue two rows of pom-pom fringe around the edge of the stool, covering the top edge of the ruffle strip.

Fringed Footstool Tuffets

Finished size: 8" x 9" x 13"

These little footstool tuffets are fun and easy to make. Shown here topped with suede and faux fur, you can use almost any fabric to cover the batting and stool top. Use upholstery tacks to secure fringe to the edges and you have a cute accessory in very little time. For an extra decorative touch, stamp the surface and add tufts with upholstery tacks.

Instructions:

1 Cut two 9" x 10" layers of batting and place on top of the stool.

2 Center the fabric over the batting, wrap the edges under the stool top and staple in place.

3 Glue bullion fringe around the edges of the stool top. Glue brush fringe on top of the bullion fringe, if desired. Referring to the photo, hammer evenly spaced upholstery tacks through the fringe header and into the stool.

Materials:

- 16" x 20" piece of suede, faux fur or fabric
- High-loft batting
- 1¼ yd. each of 6" bullion fringe and brush fringe (optional)
- 8" x 9" x 10" footstool
- Permanent fabric adhesive
- Upholstery tacks
- Heavy-duty staple gun
- Hammer

Juice Can Tuffet

Finished size: 8" x 14"

This little tuffet made from juice cans is one of my favorites, mostly because it's fashioned like one my grandmother, "Mamaw," made in the '30s. My mother and I put our heads together trying to figure out how she made it, and I think we came pretty close. Although I doubt there was super glue to hold the cans together back then, E-6000 does the trick these days. Assign your family the job of drinking seven large cans of juice or punch, and you're ready to go.

Materials:

- ½ yd. floral
- ½ yd. stripe
- Batting: low-loft cotton for covering tuffet; high-loft polyester to pad top
- 1½ yd. each of tasseled fringe with decorative header
- Seven large juice cans (Hi-C, etc.)
- E-6000 adhesive
- Permanent fabric adhesive
- 14" circle of cardboard
- Punch-style can opener
- Tracing paper

Instructions:

1 Open each can using a punch-style can opener to make two holes; do not remove the end of the can.

Gluing cans

Glue cans together as shown.

Empty the cans, rinse and let dry. Arrange the cans as shown and glue the edges together with E-6000 adhesive. Let the glue dry overnight.

2 Trace the outline of the cans onto the cardboard and cut out for the tuffet bottom. To make a pattern for the top and bottom fabric panels, trace the outline onto tracing paper, add 2" to the edges and cut out.

3 To make a pattern for the top and bottom of the tuffet, trace the outline of the cans onto tracing paper; add 2" to the edges and cut out.

4 Using the tracing paper pattern, cut two panels from the floral print and one each from the cotton and polyester battings.

5 From the stripe fabric and cotton batting each, cut one 9" x 48" strip for the sides.

6 Use fabric adhesive for all remaining gluing. To pad the assembled cans, center and glue the shaped batting panels to the tops. Clip the inside corners on the excess batting and glue to the sides of the cans, easing the curves smoothly.

7 With the upper edges aligned, glue the batting strip around the sides of the cans. Clip the excess fabric at the lower edge and glue to the bottom of the cans.

8 Glue one floral panel to the top and the stripe panel to the sides, turning under and gluing the raw edge to end the strip.

9 Center and glue the remaining floral panel to the cardboard bottom piece. Clip the excess fabric edges to the cardboard and glue to the back. With the covered side out, glue the covered cardboard to the bottom of the cans.

10 Glue the tasseled fringe around the upper edge of the tuffet.

Patterns

Chenille By The Inch Leaf & Flower Patterns

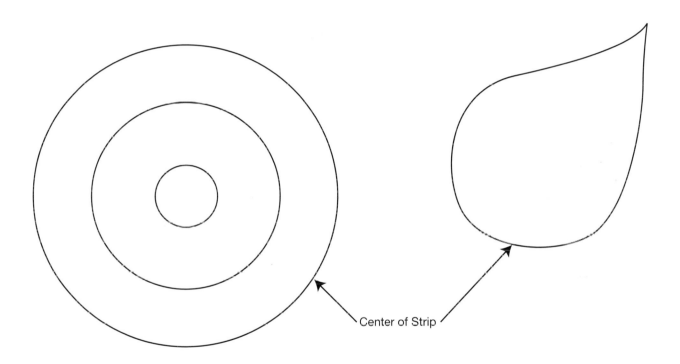

Center of Strip

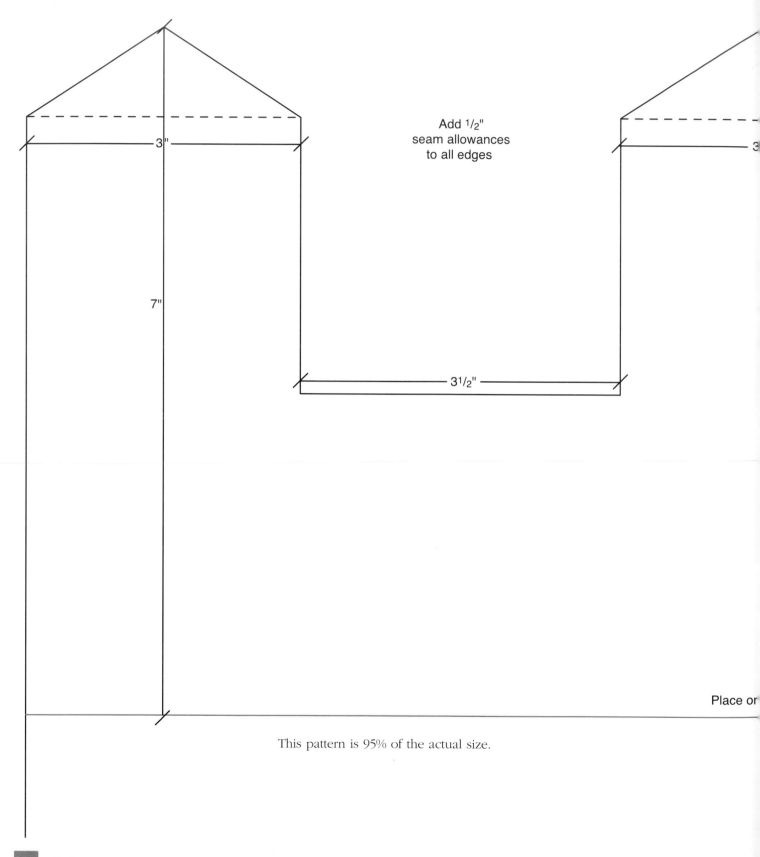

Add ¹/₂"
seam allowances
to all edges

3"

7"

3¹/₂"

Place or

This pattern is 95% of the actual size.

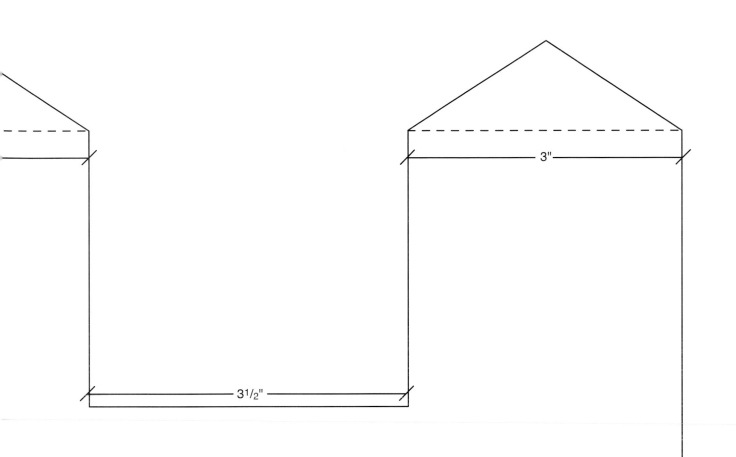

3"

3¹/₂"

This pattern is 95% of the actual size.

Couched Fall Leaves Pattern

Dog Bone Appliqué Pattern

Credits and Resources

Thank you to the following companies and artists for their contributions. Refer to the Web sites or call the number given for more information.

GENERAL SUPPLIES

Beacon Adhesives™
www.beaconcreates.com
Fabri-Tac® permanent fabric adhesive.

Crowning Touch
www.fasturnjunction.com
800-729-0280
Fasturn® tube-turning tools.

Fairfield Processing
www.poly-fil.com
800-980-8000
Soft Touch® pillow and cushion forms; Nu-Foam® foam alternative; Poly-fil®Polyester Fiberfill; Poly-fil® Ultra-Loft® and Natural Cotton®Batting.

Hollywood Trims/Prym Dritz
www.prymdritz.com
Cotton filler cord.

Husqvarna Viking Sewing Machine Co.
www.husqvarnaviking.com
800-758-3742
Designer I Sewing Machine and accessory feet; 936 Serger.

Jackman's Fabrics
www.jackmansfabrics.com
800-758-3742
Pillow templates; upholstery supplies; sewing notions.

June Tailor
www.junetailor.com
800-844-5400
Fusible Batting; Colorfast Printer Fabric™; Quilter's Cut 'n Press II™.

Kandi Corp.
www.KandiCorp.com
Heat-fix crystals; Applicator wand.

Prym Dritz
www.prymdritz.com
Omnigrid acrylic rulers; rotary cutter and scissors; Compass Points; Wonder Tape self-adhesive; double-sided basting tape; Mark-B-Gone fabric markers; Covered Buttons; Fray Check seam sealant; Heavy-duty staple gun and staples; Interior Expressions upholstery needles; upholstery zippers and waxed button thread.

Purrfections Artistic Wearables
www.purrfections.com
800-691-4293
Pelle's See Thru Stamps™; textile paint; stamp pad

Therm O Web
www.thermoweb.com
HEATnBOND® iron-on adhesive sheets.

FABRICS

Covington/Spectrum Fabrics
Ask retailer to order.
Chicken Toile Pillow; Outdoor Cushions; Puffy Tuffet; Floral Tuffet with Painted Feet.

Dan River
Ask retailer to order.
Chair Cushion with Prairie Points, background; Fitted Stool Cushion with Ruffle, ruffle.

Exotic Silks/Thai Silks
www.thaisilks.com
800-722-7455
Tufted Flowers Pillows; Framed Photo Transfer Pillow; Button-On Reversible Topper Pillow; Couched Ultrasuede on Silk Pillows; Tufted Knife Edge Floor Pillow; Box Edge Floor Pillow.

Jackman's Fabrics

See "General Supplies" information.

Cover projects; On-point Panels Pillows; Pieced Border Panels Pillows; Reversible Envelope Flap Pillow; Ribbon Trimmed Bee Pillow; Palm Tree Diamonds Pillow; Pleated Ruffle Chair Cushion; Ruffled Stool Cushion; Chair Cushion with Ruched Edge; Floral Tuffet with Pleated Skirt; Mitered Stripe Tuffet.

Linda Kubik, Elements Patterns

509-659-0209

Handwoven Pillows.

Logantex Fabrics

Ask retailer to order.

Faux Fur Footstool Tuffet.

Rebecca Yaffe Textile Design

www.rebeccayaffe.com

Handpainted Silk Pillow with Suede Center.

The Leather Factory/Tandy Leather Co.

www.tandyleather.com

888-890-1611

Suede Footstool Tuffet.

Toray Ultrasuede America

Ask retailer to order.

Couched Ultrasuede on Silk Pillows; Handpainted Raw Silk with Suede Center.

Waverly

www.waverly.com

Bedroom Ensemble: Pillows; Pillow Shams; Duvet Cover and Juice Can Tuffet; Looped Corners Pillow; Toile Circle Panel Pillow toile; Chair Cushion with Prairie Points toile; Tufted Stool Cushion with Chair Ties; Fitted Stool Cushion with Ruffle; Dog Bed Cushion; Dining Chair with Permanent Cushion; Blue Stripe Tuffet; Storage Tuffet.

TRIMS

Conso Trims

Available at fabric stores.

Bedroom Ensemble; Looped Corners Pillow; Tufted Rectangular Tuffet; Storage Tuffet with Lid; Suede Footstool Tuffet.

Expo International

www.expointl.com

800-772-7525

Chicken Toile Pillow with Feather Trim.

Fabric Café™

www.fabriccafe.com

903-509-5999

Chenille Pillow and Tuffet, Chenille By The Inch™.

Hollywood Trims/Prym Dritz

See "General Supplies" information.

Trim Transformations Pillow; Chenille Pillow and Tuffet, pom-pom trim; Rounded Floral Tuffet with Painted Feet; Faux Fur Tuffet.

Jackman's Fabrics

See "General Supplies" information

Same projects as fabrics.

Sally Houk Exclusives

www.picturetrail.com/sallyhoukexclusives

419-347-7969

Double Flange Pillow; Tapestry Pillow; Place Mat Pillow.

Wright's

www.wrights.com

Tufted Stool Cushion with Chair Ties.

BUTTONS AND BEADS

Emerald's Beads
EmeraldStacy@hotmail.com
360-786-8851
Trim Transformations Pillow beads.

Rama Raku Buttons
elensul@hotmail.com
360-786-8851
Trim Transformations Pillow button; Button-On Reversible Topper Pillow buttons; Painted Silk Pillow with Suede Center buttons; Handwoven Envelope Pillow buttons.

Worldly Goods Buttons
www.worldlygoodsbuttons.com
541-488-7881
Vintage Handkerchief Pillow buttons; Banded Button Closure Pillow buttons; Tufted Knife Edge Floor Pillow buttons.

PUBLICATIONS

Creative Machine Embroidery magazine
Subscriptions: www.cmemag.com
800-677-5212
Embroidered Silk Pillows; Embroidered Bench Top.

Sew News magazine
Subscriptions: www.sewnews.com
800-289-6397
Tropical Vase Pillow; Monkey Pillow; Couched Ultrasuede Leaves Pillow.

ABOUT THE AUTHOR

Carol Zentgraf is a designer and writer specializing in sewing, fabrics, decorating, and painting. She has a degree in interior design and commercial art from Drake University. Carol has worked in the craft and sewing publishing industry for 25 years, most recently as the fabric editor for Sew News magazine. Her designs and articles have been published in a number of books and magazines, including *Sew News, Better Homes and Gardens Simply Creative Sewing, Creative Machine Embroidery, and McCall's Quick Quilts.* She lives in Peoria, Illinois with her husband, Dave, and has two grown children, Dan and Carolyn.